Advance Praise for
Dial Down: Holistic Strategies to Move from Chaos to Calm

"Thought-provoking tools to help navigate the many challenges life can present."
~ Major Oprah Odugbela
U.S. Air Force and Family Nurse Practitioner

"Encouraging and inspiring, this book offers practical tips and authentic insights on finding peace and balance amidst chaos. A must-read for anyone seeking calmness and grounding in their lives."
~ Rachel Draxler
Principal Fraud Investigator

"Where were these tools when I was a young firefighter? I feel that first responders and military members will benefit from learning these methods of releasing from the chaos of our jobs both in the short and long term."
~ Michael Hook
Fire Captain (ret.) and U.S. Navy veteran

"An organic, compelling collection of real-life challenges and triumphs showing that we can impact ourselves and others in immeasurable ways. *Dial Down* instills the valuable lesson of how important true connection is. It compels us to learn to cherish, protect, and support the ones we love, including ourselves."
~ Joe's Legacy: Ciera Durden, Karli Durden Nelson, and Jake Durden

Dial Down:
Holistic Strategies to Move from Chaos to Calm

Dial Down:
Holistic Strategies to Move from Chaos to Calm

Raquel Durden

Two Rivers, Wisconsin

Copyright © 2025 Raquel Durden
All rights reserved

Fresh Water Press, LLC
PO Box 425
Two Rivers, WI 54241

Cover design by Vagabond Creative Studio
Author Photograph by Martina Schmidt

ISBN: 979-8-9912318-5-5

Library of Congress Number: 2025936618

Please note the information contained within this document is for educational and informational purposes only. The content of this book is not meant to substitute for the advice of a licensed professional or trained healthcare professional. If expert assistance is required, the services of a professional should be sought. The author and publisher specifically disclaim any liability incurred from the use or application of the contents of this book.

Certain names and identifying details have been changed to protect the privacy and security of the individuals.

This book is dedicated to:

All who serve! Thank you for facing the chaos of our world. May you always find calm to live in balance for yourselves and those who love you. You are seen, valued, appreciated, and resilient.

And my son, Sergeant Tyler Durden, who carries a quiet strength—always calm, generous, and supportive of others. I give a nod to your incredible resilience, kind spirit, and protective nature.

Foreword

How do you come down to a soft landing? For paratroopers like Raquel and me, you understand after stepping out of the aircraft you are going to the ground one way or another. We train and prepare for contingencies and know that the hard landings are more frequent than not. Those hard landings add up over time and much like a life of service, there are hidden costs. The weight of responsibility and leadership takes its toll, yet we push forward without pause. The charges add up while we neglect our own well-being.

Raquel's book, *Dial Down: Holistic Strategies to Move from Chaos to Calm*, is a guide to thriving, not just surviving the hidden challenges. She offers simple, practical tools grounded in holistic wellness that will prepare you for a soft landing from the hard parts of life. The stories are real, the prescription works, and you just need to take the first step.

Raquel and I served together for several years in and out of the Army. She has an innate ability to develop people and deliver results. Whether she is working in recruiting, for intelligence, in a joint and coalition force in Africa, or with health care providers during the COVID-19 pandemic, I've seen how her passion for people sets the conditions for individual and organizational excellence. This book is a fusion of her experiences and provides a framework for self-development.

This isn't just a guide; it's a collection of real stories from those who have faced challenges and turned inward to restore their strength. Raquel presents these personal stories with practical advice on yoga, breathwork, journaling, nutrition, and prayer, making this an interactive and easy-to-follow resource. As warriors and leaders, we know the value of discipline and strategy. *Dial Down* reminds us that hard landings happen, the hidden costs are real, and there are proven methods to overcome challenges and be your best.

If you're ready to embrace positive change, this is your book. Read it. Use it. And take that next step toward a better, more balanced life.

— Peter C. VanAmburgh, Ed.D, Colonel (U.S. Army Retired)
Author of *One Mission to Africa, Leadership Lessons for a Lifetime*

INTRODUCTION
A Guide to Grounded Living

In a world that often feels noisy, relentless, and chaotic, *Dial Down: Holistic Strategies to Move from Chaos to Calm* offers a path to stillness, balance, and clarity. I am a retired U.S. Army Lieutenant Colonel, combat veteran, paratrooper, and advanced-stage cancer survivor. In my retirement, I co-founded a nonprofit organization serving women veterans and first responders. With my wealth of experience and unshakable resilience, I provide actionable, evidence-based, and experiential tools to help readers navigate life's challenges with calm and renewed strength. I have faced my own profound moments of chaos.

One such experience occurred in the aftermath of 9/11, when I was assigned as a Casualty Assistance Officer (CAO) at the Pentagon crash site. I served as a personal liaison to a victim's family, helping ease the heavy burden of identification, burial, and benefits. My first task was to ask the victim's family to gather personal items—toothbrush, hairbrush, and razor—for DNA identification.

One morning during this assignment, I encountered a search team composed largely of military band members—musicians who had been repurposed as responders. The team's mission was to search for the "ABCs," a stark, operational term for Airplane, Body, and Computer parts. The search team wore makeshift hazmat suits crafted from disposable hospital scrubs, gas masks, and duct tape sealing their wrists and ankles.

The air was thick with the acrid stench of burning JP-8 airplane fuel, a smell that lingered for weeks and remains a powerful trigger for me to this day. I recall that the smell alone was overwhelming, but the weight of the task was vast. Because I held a top-secret security clearance, I was given an additional duty to my CAO role. I was charged with gathering and securing any classified documents the search team recovered from the wreckage, safeguarding sensitive information amid unimaginable destruction.

Such moments stay with a person, reshaping their understanding of resilience and survival making me question how do people process experiences like these and how do they overcome the triggers that linger long after the chaos has passed.

My own journey has taught me that even in the face of chaos, grounding practices are essential for reclaiming calm. At its core, *Dial Down* incorporates personal stories from individuals in high-stress professions including military personnel, first responders, and emergency room nurses, who have used these tools to regain and continuously access their inner calm through "story boards" presented in the book. The contributors share their journey toward crafting a personal mantra, a simple yet powerful mindfulness tool they rely on to center themselves. Interspersed with these inspiring stories are chapters introducing holistic practices such as yoga, nature immersion, journaling, plant-based eating, and prayer.

This book is an invitation to learn, engage, and grow. It is designed as an interactive guide, encouraging readers to reflect on their experiences and incorporate these wellness practices into their life. This book is a tool to return to as often as needed. Each chapter provides practical strategies to enhance self-awareness, foster connection, and thrive despite life's inevitable stressors. Think of *Dial Down* as your personal wellness toolkit, a transformational guide to grounding yourself and thriving in the face of personal challenges and the chaos of our shared world.

The after-tax proceeds from *Dial Down* will support organizations and good causes dedicated to advancing holistic wellness practices and fostering meaningful connections for those who need them most. This commitment amplifies the book's mission of promoting healing, resilience, and connection, ensuring its impact extends far beyond the written page.

How to Use this Book

There is no single "right" way to navigate *Dial Down*. Whether you read it cover to cover or dive into the chapters that resonate most, this book is here to meet you exactly where you are. Here is how to make the most of it:

1. **Read with Reflection:** take your time with each chapter. Highlight passages, underline key points, and jot down thoughts in the margins. Pause often to reflect on how each wellness practice or personal story speaks to your unique life experiences and challenges. By engaging actively with the content, you will create a personal connection that deepens your understanding.

2. **Engage with the Exercises:** Each chapter introduces a wellness practice, explains its benefits, and walks you through step-by-step guide to incorporate these practices into your life. These exercises encourage you to turn inward and take actionable steps toward cultivating calm. Pay close attention to the personal stories. Each one offers relatable perspectives and motivation for embracing these practices in your own life.

3. **Craft your Own Journey:** Reflective prompts and poetry exercises guide you in creating a personal mantra and a tailored wellness routine. What works for one person may not work for another. This book empowers you to design strategies that truly fit your unique needs.

4. **Keep it Close:** As life evolves, so will your wellness needs. Keep this book nearby as a trusted resource to revisit whenever you feel overwhelmed, unbalanced, or in need of grounding. It's a living guide that grows with you, offering fresh insights and reminders as you face new challenges and seasons of life. If you are reading this as an e-book, consider pairing it with a hard copy to fully engage with the reflective exercises and personalized notes.

Dial Down is more than a book. It is a companion for your wellness journey. Whether you are seeking calm amidst the chaos or striving to deepen your connection to yourself and others, this guide offers the tools, inspiration, and encouragement to flourish.

With reflection and practice, you will learn how to move from chaos to calm and embrace a life grounded in resilience and balance. Read on!

The Framework of Dial Down

This book is designed to help you move from reflection to action. It is built for busy people, blending inspiration with practical tools you can use immediately. The framework includes:

1. **Personal stories**: Each real-life story is from an individual who has faced chaos head-on. Each story depicts how the writer moved through chaos and uncovered a personal grounding anchor. Each anchor begins with a vivid image of a memory from a real place that centers them. Using a simple, yet profound, cinquain poetry framework, we worked together to develop a memorable mantra linked to an anchor, helping to access calm wherever and whenever needed. These stories demonstrate the transformative power of turning inward and show that inner calm is not reserved for the few but is available to anyone willing to seek it.

2. **Holistic wellness practices:** In addition to the personal stories are chapters that introduce evidence-based wellness strategies. From yoga and nature immersion to plant-based eating, journaling and prayer, each practice is explained with step-by-step guidance, real-world benefits, and tips for integration. These insights are drawn from my personal experience, my work with veterans and first responders, and proven strategies. Each practice is presented in a practical way to show how it can transform lives.

3. **Interactive tools:** Throughout the book, you will have opportunities to create your own grounding anchor, personal mantra, and weekly wellness routine. Reflective questions and exercises help you connect to your inner calm repeatedly, just as others have done. You also will

find space to explore how these practices can naturally fit into your life, making them easily accessible rather than overwhelming.

Together, these elements create a rhythm that is engaging and practical. By the end of the book, you will not just have read inspiring stories; you will have built a personalized toolkit to support your journey toward calm and resilience.

Introducing the Storyboards

Central to *Dial Down* are its storyboards—visual and written reflections of each person's journey from chaos to calm. These storyboards offer glimpses into the private thoughts and experiences of everyday heroes highlighting military personnel, first responders, and an emergency room nurse, who serve our communities and nation. They illustrate how individuals facing immense pressure find their way to a calm center.

But these are not just stories to admire. Each storyboard serves as a template, showing that anyone, regardless of circumstances, can craft tools to navigate chaos and find peace. Each storyboard captures:

- **Chaos:** A brief overview of the challenges they faced, providing context and highlighting the universality of chaos.

- **An Anchor:** A visual representation of their grounding anchor, a vivid image and memory of a real place that centers them. These anchors are personal but accessible, inviting readers to connect with the concept.

- **Calm:** The transformation achieved through their mantra practice. Using a Cinquain poem structure resulting in a single unique word, they can now use to access calm regularly and on demand.

Think of these storyboards as both inspirational and instructional, helping you see how to navigate your unique challenges and build inner resilience. An example of a storyboard follows.

Tim's Storyboard ~ The Rooftop

Chaos	Post Deployment Anxiety
Anchor	Coastline Image
Calm	Personal Mantra of "Order"

With expertise in defense counterterrorism in North Africa, I found myself on a forward deployed rotation to support a special mission unit. During my watch, an attack occurred at the Radisson Blu Hotel in Bamako, Mali. A terrorist group had gone into the luxury hotel shooting. The American operator, who immediately responded and went in first, was my teammate and friend. Never in my military service had I experienced or heard of anyone going into a crisis solo. The Army had always drilled into me to have a buddy, work as part of a team.

My commanding officer said, "Hey Tim, I need everything you've got on this event."

I knew immediately that this was a high-stakes situation—an ambush. At the time, the event hadn't yet made the news. CNN wouldn't report it for several hours. My command received approval to act before any other units in the area or even the American embassy. The chaos for me was the realization that this was real—someone I knew was actively involved. A friend of mine was running toward danger—a terrorist attack and hostage crisis.

I had been deployed to provide intelligence; I am not a shooter. I served as the senior intel analyst on a team of eight. We had to provide the best possible intel to support the operators on the ground. My team and I canvassed open-source information resources to build an accurate picture of what my teammate was walking into.

We scoured Google Periscope (a live feed capability which was shut down in 2021), Twitter, and any other open-source channels for details. I knew there was limited intelligence, surveillance, reconnaissance, and medical assets.

My mind was racing, but I stayed focused on my boss's words: "Give me everything you've got, Tim. Paint an accurate picture of what's going on so we can best support the ground forces and the host nation."

Like most initial reports, the first intel we received was incomplete and mostly wrong. Soon, we learned and confirmed that six Americans were held at the hotel. This attack occurred just after the Benghazi incident, where our nation's response time had lagged. There was a deep, collective effort not to let that happen again. The stress of working through every angle to build a solid, accurate picture was enormous. At one point, communications went dark for two hours. I didn't know the status of my friend. When he came back online, he urgently requested more resources and additional teammates. He ultimately got them.

This wasn't a named operation with a playbook or a battle drill. This was a real-time response to a terrorist attack and hostage crisis. My boss gave us time and resources so my team and I could do our best work. Even in a climate-controlled room, the oppressive heat and unrelenting pressure of that crisis is seared into my memory.

# # # #

My mentoring relationship began with Tim when I accepted him into my unit as the new Second Lieutenant. Over the years, our bond has grown, and our relationship feels like family. He knew the emphasis and value I put on decompressing after a mission.

The rising sun warms Tim's shoulders and the back of his head as he sits on the well-worn lounge chair perched on the rooftop. As the sun climbs, birds call, and Tim watches the shadows disappear, revealing the glistening seawater of the Amalfi Coast. Having completed the most exceptional overseas mission of his Army career, Tim still feels responsibility for the baton he handed to the incoming team chief.

The experience was electrifying, everything felt so bright and daring. Being a part of global civilization was his adventure. After six months of being amped up and hypervigilant, Tim feels twinges of relief in being alone while gazing at the limitless water below. He no longer needs to search for overt threats and hidden terrors.

Tim starts to feel how small and insignificant we all are—tiny wheels in the big wheel of life. His days start earlier with a run in the sleepy stillness of off-season Sorento. The bustling beach town is cleansed of tourists, trash trucks, and absurd smells. There is no artificial commotion, only locals tending to their own errands.

Thankfully, when he runs there are no noises of cars backfiring or angry mufflers. It smells peaceful. It is peaceful. It is discoverable! Tim hears the silence that is his own heartbeat, breath, and cadence of his pace as he runs parallel to the attentive shoreline. As a seasoned runner, he moves with a gazelle-like ease, feeling the wind on his face. His feet move swiftly and there is no need to look down or worry. He trusts his sure footing and senses the newness all around.

When he returns to his hotel calmer, he finds his wife still sleeping. He makes his post-run coffee enjoying it at the perfect temperature with a dusting of raw sugar.

He laughs to himself, "Artistry in a cup."

Then, he heads up to the rooftop. Seated comfortably and sipping his brew, a new awareness of gratefulness and humility arises. The ability and opportunity to sit in this nature-blessed, seemingly perfectly, safe space fills his awareness during these times.

Tim, a black man from humble roots, shared, "My demographics don't trend to being a world traveler and to being able to take my wife."

This experience feels both real and surreal. Every time Tim thought about this memory, a picture of a better life emerges.

"Were those seagulls?" he wonders.

After his most recent memory of the Amalfi Coast, they come into focus as seagulls. The added details become his new memory. Tim visits this peaceful safe space, his grounding anchor, to loosen the vise on his breath, memories, and mental traffic.

With his chaotic past and thoughts always pushing past the limits of performative roles and concerns, Tim regularly seeks solace near water. For him, water has its own order and renews his belief in a heavenly Creator. A deeper exhale and resetting solitude are his peaceful prizes to enjoy—no sharing or justifying.

Near water, he realizes things are not as big or busy as they seem. There are battle buddies for action, accountability, and camaraderie, but people need alone time too. Feeling the relief of being alone but not lonely, Tim relaxes into his rooftop view of the water . . . his water.

Poem
Rooftop
Unobstructed view
Glistening, exploring, limitless
Unsolicited warmth and peace
Order

Mantra
Order

Tim's personal mantra is the word order. By quietly revisiting his mantra whenever he needs a moment of calm, Tim can cultivate a sense of grounding.

Table of Contents

Foreword i
Introduction: A Guide to Grounded Living iii
   Tim's Storyboard: The Rooftop viii

Chapter 1: Navigating Chaos 1
   Brandon's Storyboard: The Deer Stand 4
Chapter 2: The Power of Connections 8
   Pam's Storyboard: The Mountain Home 20
Chapter 3: Breathe In, Let Go 24
   James's Storyboard: The Porch 41
Chapter 4: Nature's Reset Button 46
   Marsha's Storyboard: The Waterfalls 59
Chapter 5: Eating For Energy and Clarity 63
   Jess's Storyboard: The Cozy Couch 77
Chapter 6: Journal Your Way to Peace 80
   Tom's Storyboard: The Water's Edge 94
Chapter 7: Prayer Power 99
   Courtney's Storyboard: Predawn Coffee 108
Chapter 8: Weaving It All Together for Balance 112
   Dave's Storyboard: The Fire Pit 122
Chapter 9: Living Your Best Dialed-Down Life 125

Appendices
   Appendix A: The Eight Limbs of Yoga 128
   Appendix B: Types of Yoga 130
   Appendix C: Personal Mantra Framework 132
   Appendix D: Color Coding 135
   Appendix E: Humble Warrior Nonprofit 136

References 140
Discussion Prompts 144
Acknowledgements 145

Chapter 1
Navigating Chaos

Chaos is everywhere. Endless responsibilities and the demands of an ever-connected society have led us to wear "busy" as a badge of honor. We often mistake constant motion for purpose or value. But what if perpetual busyness isn't a mark of success, but rather a response to stress? The chaos we cling to is often just a thin, fragile shield, hiding the deeper emotional and physical tolls of life.

Unknowingly, I lived this way for years. Outwardly, I embodied health and achievement. As a combat veteran with a thriving career, a devoted wife and mother, an athlete competing in triathlons, and someone leading a lifestyle many would deem exemplary, I seemed to have it all together. But inside, my body was fighting a silent battle. I wasn't aware. At age 47, I was diagnosed with advanced-stage endometrioid cancer—a type of uterine cancer. I was told that the five-year survival rate was fifty-seven percent. I was forced to dial down and confront a reality I had never anticipated.

The world had conditioned me to be, know, and constantly do. My background in athletics and military service sharpened my ability to push through challenges, succeed, and persevere. So, my instinctive response to hardship was to push myself harder. Combat deployments, parachuting out of planes, and even cancer did not stop me. Well, at least not outwardly. After much deliberation, I chose the traditional treatments of surgery and chemotherapy as the accepted recipe for living.

However, the physical, mental, and emotional toll of these cancer treatments were staggering. I realized I needed natural, gentler treatment, but the way forward was not clear and seemed risky. Up until this point in my life, I had regularly turned to a handful of healthy habits like running, the occasional yoga class, and prayer for resilience. I soon learned from my medical team that these habits were considered complementary treatments. My cancer journey is best described as discovery learning. I read multiple books, reviewed clinical studies, and actively sought advice from medical professionals and insights from other cancer survivors. Gathering information and exploring holistic options was not stressful; it comforted me. By nature, I am an enthusiastic encourager. Throughout the process of self-directed learning, I explored different approaches, deepened my understanding, and gained confidence in my decisions. With excitement, I wove together a personal holistic wellness plan. Inspired by how much better I felt, I eagerly shared my journey with others. It was not until I transitioned into survivorship and fully embraced holistic wellness that I realized chaos is not something to fix, avoid, or fear. Chaos is something to navigate.

Over time, I discovered simple strategies and comforting tools that helped me dial down the noise of life and find calm in any storm. I came to see that calm is not just an occasional refuge but a state I can access consistently by putting these practices into action. I found myself eagerly sharing this knowledge with anyone navigating a new cancer diagnosis, battling disease, or facing chaos in their lives. I fully believed these practices could offer them the same sense of calm and hope I had found.

Quickly, I noticed that those who adopted my suggested holistic practices appreciated the connection and found empowerment in having tangible actions they could take. I saw their mood shift from being overwhelmed to becoming active participants in their chaotic journey rather than feeling powerless.

This realization transformed my life inspiring me to obtain holistic certifications and co-found the nonprofit organization: Humble Warrior Wellness & Yoga, Inc. For nearly a decade, my nonprofit has served veterans and first responders, primarily in Georgia and Wisconsin, where I am deeply connected. By sharing the two pillars of connection and holistic wellness, we have enhanced well-being, reduced social isolation, and supported the prevention of suicide.

This book is my way of sharing transformational tools, insights, and practices with the greater community. I openly share what I know, how I live, and what I have taught others through my nonprofit and personal relationships. This book is for anyone seeking calm amidst life's inevitable challenges, no matter what form your chaos may take.

Why Now?

Most of us wait for a breaking point before prioritizing our well-being. But what if you did not have to? What if small, meaningful steps today could prevent long-term consequences of stress tomorrow? Do not wait for a disease, diagnosis, or disaster to force change. Let this book of holistic wellness strategies guide you toward positive transformation now.

Dial Down is not about fixing what's wrong with you. This book is about nurturing what is already right within you. Using the tools and stories in this book, you will learn to:

- Embrace stillness in a fast-paced world.
- Develop resilience to life's challenges.
- Build a wellness routine that evolves with you.

The journey begins here. Together, let's move from chaos to calm and intentionally create a grounded, balanced life. Let this book serve as your trusted guide as you uncover your path to calm.

Navigating Chaos Reflection Questions:

1. How do you navigate chaos in your life?

2. What is your grounding anchor—a vivid image and memory of a real place that helps to center you?

BRANDON'S STORYBOARD
The Deer Stand

Chaos	Dangerous Rescue Mission
Anchor	Deer Stand
Calm	Personal Mantra of "Solitude"

The call I responded to while serving on a swift water team stands out as one of the most chaotic times of my career. It was a flash flood, and our team was called in to help. We had four guys in a truck towing our boat, and I was the rescue swimmer. A command vehicle led the way to the incident site. We quickly assessed there were four teenagers stuck on the ledge of a concrete mill. But it wasn't just them, we also had an adult and a seven-year-old stranded near a dam, with water cresting over the edge like a waterfall. The adult was the uncle, and the young boy was his nephew.

I quickly realized that to execute a successful rescue, I'd need to navigate at least seven or eight different water currents. It was the only time in twenty years that I stopped in action to pray. I was genuinely afraid for my safety too. I took a moment to access the currents and plan my approach. The teens were in immediate danger, but the situation with the uncle and nephew was worse. There was no way to swim through to reach them.

I had to think quickly and shift my strategy. First, we decided to rescue the four teenagers with ropes and personal flotation devices. My teammates slid the floatation devices down by rope and had each team member jump into an eddy, a circular movement of water causing a small whirlpool among the raging water. One by one, we pulled the teenagers out.

Later, while watching the news, I realized that I was the one catching the victims as they jumped off the ledge. The dam was still roaring, and the water kept rising, but we had to get the uncle and nephew out.

My team then climbed upstream along the bank to rescue them, with the 7-year-old boy being pulled out first. The uncle had to throw a rope loop around his nephew and throw him upstream. That moment was the most dangerous.

I couldn't help but think, "What if the uncle slips?"

When it was over, the enormity of the high-risk successful rescue hit me like a wave. It was the biggest adrenaline dump I can ever remember. I dropped the top of my wetsuit, laid down in the parking lot, and just stared at the sky for five minutes. From the time our feet hit the shore to the completion of the rescue was only 25 minutes. But the chaos, danger, and rush of the experience will stay with me forever.

# # # #

I began to with work Brandon after meeting him through his wife, a fellow yoga teacher. With so much responsibility and pressure in his work, I noticed it was challenging for him to be still.

Constantly engaged in the busy hive-like atmosphere of Fire Station 12, Brandon was accustomed to being primed with his protective and lifesaving gear perfectly postured for the next call, crisis, or proverbial cat stuck in a tree. Couple his first responder status with an active family that fills and spills over his household; he was and is always on.

So many roles, responsibilities, and titles . . . veteran, firefighter, driver, husband, father, friend, and more. The call of the world was high pitched and deafening. Too acquainted with trauma and loss, he responded with purpose, precision, and an air tank of humility.

Craving stillness, Brandon heads to his friend Barber's hunting property in Madison County, Georgia. The closer to deer season, the more the call to come sit in his stand intensifies and echoes. Just knowing the view exists calms his senses.

Brandon feels a shift in his deep self and silently shouts, "Shit yeah, I'm going to the property!"

There is preparation to do. He mows the target area and gathers provisions.

"No one else hunts my stand," declares Brandon solemnly. "I share everything, my home with my loving family, and even my bunk with two teammates on different shifts." He reminds himself, "It's important that I have something—my own space, that's just mine."

Convinced, he heads out to his stand. Alone with the morning sunrise on his shoulders, he carries a Browning X-bolt 270 hunting rifle, snacks, and a full water bottle. Layered up, he sports woodland camouflage coveralls, a long sleeve moisture-wicking dark shirt, thermals, well-worn rubber boots, thick socks, scarred up gloves, and a hat.

As he walks five hundred yards from the truck, the grind and noise of the world fade and nature begins to whisper, "Time to be still."

As squirrels scurry and birds chirp, Brandon ascends the pine tree to reach his own perch. He carefully pivots away from facing the tree bark, softens his silhouette, and settles into the netted, padded seat of his deer stand. In contrast, his strong forearms rest on narrow metal rails with the cold rifle positioned across his lap in the ready position.

"My favorite mornings are when it's cold, because I hate bugs."

The cold is incredibly calming to him. The fallen leaves and dead underbrush provide an expansive portal of the forest. An hour in, the taste of coffee and the juice of pungent Redman lingered on his tongue. Brandon inhales the cool, damp air and exhales as if he could watch squirrels play and deer meander all day.

Mentally humming, "I get a peaceful easy feeling" by the Eagles, Brandon releases the threat of being behind schedule. Brandon savors the stillness of sitting and felt the ease of being alone but not lonely. As he looks around, his main thought is, "God made this."

No one needs rescue, Brandon concludes. With heaven hidden in his heart, Brandon knows he is protected and connected in his deer stand. His soul comfortably shines, and for a time there is no buzzing, only comforting solitude.

Poem
Stillness
peaceful pines
connecting, whispering, resetting
too acquainted with loss
solitude

Mantra
"Solitude"

Brandon's personal mantra is the word solitude. By quietly revisiting his mantra whenever he needs a moment of calm, Brandon can cultivate a sense of grounding.

CHAPTER 2
The Power of Connections

Connection is not just a desire—it is a human necessity. Cultivating strong, supportive connections is a lifelong, important holistic wellness practice to enhance your overall well-being. As children, we seek someone to play with; as teenagers, we pick our peer group; and as adults, we may find ourselves searching for a life partner.

Why? Our constitution demands social contact and the need to belong is a primary human motivation (Shovestul, et al. 2020). Supportive family, friends, and colleagues can guide us in life's challenges, join us in celebrating our successes, and share in our daily activities. Think of the joy you feel when connecting with a bestie over lunch, getting a text from your favorite family member, or celebrating a successful milestone with your inner circle.

The term connection broadly refers to a sense of association or relationship with another person—family, friend, or colleague. Connection may involve the sharing of thoughts, emotions, and shared experiences that foster a sense of trust, belonging, and support. Similarly, social connection refers to the interactions or relationships we have with groups, the broader community, or society. Social connections may encompass a sense of belonging, emotional closeness, or feeling understood.

Reasons to Connect

Positive connections, whether a supportive relationship or a strong network, enhance our well-being. The Center for Disease Control notes that social connections are key in promoting overall health, as supportive networks contribute to emotional resilience, reduce stress, and even impact physical health by lowering risks for conditions like heart disease and depression (Centers for Disease Control and Prevention 2024).

Dr. Amy Stevens, a U.S. Navy veteran, licensed professional counselor, Humble Warrior Wellness & Yoga partner, and founder of Georgia Military Women (GMW)—the largest and most diverse social group of women veterans in the State of Georgia—is passionate about the role of social connection in the mental health and well-being of the veteran community. She explains,

> "Positive connections help create a buffer against feelings of isolation and depression. A strong network provides both validation and a sense of safety, fundamental components for mental well-being.
>
> Positive relationships can be a powerful form of suicide prevention. As a clinician, many of the individuals I work with come to me feeling isolated either due to post-traumatic stress reintegration challenges, or a sense of disconnection from their peers and families. Veterans in the counseling room are like most other clients. The difference is that they have lost the strength of the military family that was once their solid foundation. Their tight-knit military family is gone, and they may be floundering to establish that same feeling of being one with others who have had similar life journeys.
>
> Women often feel especially disconnected—not only from civilian society but also from the military community they once knew. Women tend not to publicly identify as veterans. We typically don't wear the ball caps and t-shirts worn by male veterans. GMW social connections provide an invaluable reminder that our experiences matter, and that we are not alone in our struggles."

GMW uses the tag line, 'Be a friend and find a friend.' Through friendships, women veterans are rediscovering their sense of self, rebuilding trust in others, and feeling empowered to thrive again. I am forever thankful for the GMW group. When Humble Warrior was merely a concept, we posted our first wellness retreat on their private Facebook page and registration for the event filled up in four hours. The desire to connect and explore wellness practices with like-minded individuals was evident. Connections provide a warm protective insulation against loneliness.

Benefits of Connecting with Others

Supportive connections benefit all of society. Dr. Stevens shares how social connections for people of all ages and stages of life offer numerous benefits, especially to veterans and first responders, who often face unique challenges due to their service experiences.

Some key benefits of being socially connected are:

> **Sense of Belonging:** Social connection fosters a sense of belonging and validation that can be life changing. Amy has seen firsthand the tremendous impact of connection in both small and large groups. In large groups, like GMW, the key benefit is the sheer diversity of lived experiences and perspectives.
>
> Dr. Stevens expresses, "You can find someone to connect with. There's power in knowing you are not alone—no matter how isolated you may feel." When it comes to small groups, Dr. Stevens comments, "The depth of connection becomes more personal. GMW holds small monthly meetups across Georgia that typically have less than fifteen attendees. These smaller, more intimate settings allow for more vulnerable sharing, which can be a key aspect of healing. Both large and small groups serve vital purposes: large groups provide broad support, while small groups foster personal transformation."
>
> In the same way, many high-capacity or multi-campus churches have adopted both large gatherings and small groups to foster deeper connections within their congregations.

➢ **Peer Support:** Connecting with others who have similar experiences can provide invaluable peer support and a network to help a person feel understood and validated. Examples of peer support groups include grief support groups for those navigating loss, cancer support groups for patients and survivors, and family-focused groups. These communities share understanding, encouragement, and practical advice tailored to unique challenges or seasons of life. Dr. Stevens has witnessed countless women veterans experience transformative changes simply through the act of connecting with others who understand their unique experiences.

She adds, "There is space for active listening, tailored support, and fostering a deeper sense of trust and safety."

Similarly, many companies have employee resource groups (ERGs) that are employee-led to foster a sense of belonging and provide support for employees with shared identities, interests, or experiences. These ERGs promote inclusivity and support a stronger organizational culture.

➢ **Increased Access to Resources:** Being socially connected increases the awareness of available resources and ability to plug into those resources, such as counseling, education, job training, or financial assistance.

Dr. Stevens stresses, "Plugging into resources and practical information is particularly important for those who feel disconnected after leaving or retiring from service. Knowing about veteran healthcare, accessing compensation for active-duty injuries, and realizing professional therapy used by other members can be helpful."

Likewise, a single parent or young family might gain access to parenting classes, affordable childcare programs, or community food pantries through connections with local support networks.

➢ **Increased Resilience:** Being connected to a community builds resilience, empowering veterans and first responders to better handle stress, trauma, and adversity.

Dr. Stevens explains a simple way for women veterans to start connecting, "Our Facebook group is an uncomplicated way to begin. They can join without any pressure to actively participate, just observing until they are ready."

For Dr. Stevens, the most rewarding moments are when members, who have been silent, take that first step toward engagement by forming friendships that are grounded in shared experience, mutual support, and healing.

➢ **Emotional Support:** People can share their experiences and challenges with others who understand, reducing feelings of isolation and loneliness. Connection provides an outlet for emotional expression and supports the prevention of suicide.

Dr. Stevens encourages veterans, as well as others, to form relationships rooted in mutual respect and understanding, where they can both offer and receive support. We all can turn to trusted friends, faith-based groups, community centers, or online support forums for emotional connection. These spaces foster understanding, offer a sense of belonging, and provide a safe outlet for sharing struggles and finding encouragement.

> **Enhanced Quality of Life:** Social connections improve overall quality of life by providing companionship, reducing loneliness, and fostering a sense of stability and fulfillment in everyday life.

Dr. Stevens feels incredibly grateful to be part of this journey with women veterans, "A new family, a new sisterhood emerges. They go from feeling forgotten or misunderstood to feeling seen and valued."

These universally applicable benefits highlight the importance of fostering strong social ties to support and enhance the overall well-being of our collective society, especially the veteran and first responder communities. It is also important to recognize that while veterans have unique experiences, the same kinds of resources are helpful to the wider community of people who also find themselves disconnected from others around them.

How to Cultivate Connections

Begin your connection practice by showing up for yourself first. Start by making intentional choices for yourself. Consider taking the first moments of the day to journal, pray, connect with an intimate partner, or have a cup of coffee. Allow yourself time to connect with your breath and thoughts. Approach your choice with a sense of mindfulness and intention, taking your time. Connecting with yourself is not a to-do list item to be checked off; allow it to become a daily ritual.

Slowly begin to expand your connections. Try drinking your coffee at a local café, walking a shelter dog, or meditating outside in the company of songbirds. Try seeking out small social opportunities. You can exchange niceties with people you see as you go about your day such as the grocery store clerk, a waiter, or the colleague you pass in the hallway.

Feeling ready to extend your connections to a social network? Try seeking out a reoccurring community gathering that sparks your interest. Since repetition builds familiarity, you may notice the regular attendees, and they will start recognizing you too.

Elyse, a YMCA Wellness Director, mother of two veterans, and Humble Warrior Wellness & Yoga supporter, attests to the phenomena of connecting regularly, "People join their local YMCA to start a journey to better themselves. After regular attendance, they begin to feel a connection, creating value beyond the benefits of regular exercise. They experience a whole body, mental, physical, and even spiritual experience by connecting to other members."

Many people find a comfortable social group through programs offered at a community center, local gym, or faith community. Being present with others regularly begins the process of fostering strong social ties.

There are many ways to seek out connections and cultivate supportive relationships. This could include joining local clubs or organizations that align with your interests, volunteering for causes you care about, or participating in group classes such as yoga or art workshops. Building connections often start with small, intentional steps toward engaging with others.

Following are intentional ways to grow your social support network (Psychological Association 2024):

> **Cast a Wide Net:** One size does not fit all; you are encouraged to look to different relationships for distinct kinds of support. Turn to people whom you can trust and count on to avoid negative interactions.
>
> Gabrielle, an experienced librarian, exemplifies "casting a wide net" by using crafting to foster community and personal connections. Professionally, she hosts monthly "Casual Crafters" sessions at her library's Makerspace. In this public space, people of all skill levels gather to work on personal projects or learn a new craft.

With free supplies and no commitment required, Gabrielle describes, "It's a judgment-free space for creativity and connection."

Personally, Gabrielle organizes monthly drop-in "crafternoons" with friends, rotating homes, sharing snacks, and enjoying each other's company while crafting or simply being present. Through these gatherings, she creates meaningful opportunities for people to connect, share, and support one another in a way that turns hobbies into heartfelt community-building.

Gabrielle shares, "The library is often seen as the hub of the community, working to bring people together to access resources and opportunities—not just books."

Consider exploring your local library's offerings.

- **Be Proactive:** You must make an effort. Try lending a hand or saying hello. When you make time for family and friends, they will be more likely to be there for you.

Elyse genuinely loves to exercise, and YMCA members see and feel her passion for exercise and people. This helps make it easier to connect with her.

Elyse shares, "When I started teaching wellness classes twenty-four years ago, I realized there were women like me who were starting a journey to better themselves. I was thankful."

Now, Elyse wants people to come for a class, a program, or social visit and just be comfortable—no judgment, no parenting responsibilities, no stress about what they need to do next. Her hope is that every person in class develops one connection, making it easier to come back.

> **Take Advantage of Technology:** When a sit-down meeting is not possible, technology allows us to connect via email, text, or video chat. Try not to rely too heavily on technology, favor face-to-face interactions.

During the COVID-19 pandemic, Elyse ensured virtual classes were available, but community connections were sorely missed.
"When COVID hit, the Y was closed for nine weeks. We had one man come every day to see if we were open. Every day! This place is unique. When a member is not in my class for a while they are missed. I try to call or text them or someone in the class will reach out and let me know what is going on with another member."

> **Follow Your Interest:** If you like to hike, sing, or play a sport, you are more likely to connect with people who like the things you like. By joining a club, taking a class, or volunteering, you can meet others who share your interests. A senior woman found her community connection in Elyse's class at the YMCA.

She wrote an appreciative email after finding the right fitness class, "What am I doing here? I am in my 60s in a low impact class. I had been an athlete, and my identity says I don't fit here. As I looked around the room, I saw a sea of women like me trying to keep up, to go to a new place, to find hope for new strength. We were all looking forward, eyes on Elyse, our instructor, ever cheerful with boundless energy, loving us, pulling fresh faith and strength out of us."

➢ **Seek Out Peer Support:** When you find yourself going through a difficult season, consider joining a support group to meet others who are dealing with similar challenges. Support groups can offer guidance when dealing with a specific stressful situation.

Living as a cancer survivor was unchartered territory for me, so I talked with my sister about joining a women's cancer support group. Jess reminded me that I needed a guide for this season of life, and though I was not an expert, there were experts out there who could help me. We laughed when she compared my life without survivorship guidance to a boat without a captain.

I finally agreed to join. I forged new friendships and benefitted from the group's collective wisdom. Support groups can be the compass that helps us navigate unfamiliar waters, showing us that we are not alone on this journey.

➢ **Improve Your Social Skills:** To get the conversational ball rolling, ask simple questions about another person. When needed, therapists can offer support as well as social anxiety and skills training.

Elyse actively works to connect the whole fitness class, "I ask questions while we are exercising, like 'Where are you from, what's your favorite food, or travel?' After every answer, someone in the class inevitably says, 'Me too!'

People open up and appreciate being seen and heard, to know they are important."

➢ **Ask For Help:** Community resources can connect you with others.

As Elyse often says, "We're all threads woven together, creating a beautiful picture of shared stories that enrich our lives."

She believes in the power of prayer and small acts of kindness, like bringing a meal or treat to let someone know they are cared for and important. If you are feeling stuck, do not hesitate to seek professional support to develop strategies for managing stress or improving social connections.

You may find camaraderie among neighbors, coworkers, friends, or family, but for some, making social connections feels daunting and uncomfortable. As the chairperson of my nonprofit, I make a significant effort to create a supportive space, free of distractions and potential triggers, where social bonds can flourish and wellness is nurtured.

To open our wellness sessions, I use intentional tools like story cards, icebreakers, and partner-based exercises to help ease stress and encourage meaningful first connections. Story cards provide gentle, visual prompts that encourage participants to share something personal in a low-pressure way—simply pick a card and share with the group the reason it resonates with you. Each card is designed to spark self-reflection and conversation. Icebreakers and partner-based exercises are interactive activities used to introduce people in a relaxed, engaging, and fun way. Afterward, we always share ways to keep building these bonds, like joining our private social media group and attending GMW meetups, which helps friendships grow beyond the program. Connecting begins with a single step and can lead to a lasting, supportive community.

Your Invitation to Connect

Understanding the value of connection highlights the importance of building strong, supportive relationships to enhance both personal and community well-being. By seeking out and nurturing meaningful connections, you can experience a wide range of benefits. You are warmly invited to create connections that matter, build relationships that uplift, and embrace a journey toward greater wellness. Step forward to connect with others and enrich your life!

Community Connections Reflection Questions:

1. How has community played a role in your wellness or life's journey?

2. What actions can you take to strengthen or create meaningful connections in your life?

PAM'S STORYBOARD
The Mountain Home

Chaos	Chronic Caregiving
Anchor	Mountain Home
Calm	Personal Mantra of "Love"

After four decades of nursing, I've witnessed shocking cases, unexpected situations, and crazy curveballs, which could challenge even the most prepared medical teams. I was trained to assess situations quickly and think ahead constantly. However, preparation doesn't guarantee control. Every time I walked into work, I knew there was always a possibility that things could go wrong.

Most days were filled with scheduled cases, unless I was on call. I remember one case vividly. My morning started off with a routine sports medicine surgery, a rotator cuff repair. The hospital was notoriously chaotic over the holidays. Patients rush to get procedures done to use their insurance benefits, and staff are often overworked and stretched thin. My patient claimed he had followed all pre-op instructions at home, including fasting. But partway through the surgery, he vomited on the operating room (OR) table. He lost his airway and nearly died. He clearly hadn't fasted as instructed. What should have been a straightforward, hour-long procedure turned into an emergency that required immediate action and a transfer to the ICU. The patient spent the night in critical condition, all because he lied.

In my line of work, things can always go sideways. People have bad reactions to anesthesia, medication, and treatment. Truly anything can happen. Why did he lie?

After the whirlwind of stabilizing and rushing him to the ICU, a fellow nurse informed me, "Pam, you've got 15 minutes to turn over the OR and get it ready for the next case."

There was no chance to catch my breath or reflect on how close we had come to losing our patient. All I could do was get it all together for my next patient. The chaos demanded my full attention, and I had to keep moving forward.

# # # #

I am very familiar with Pam, now a Humble Warrior volunteer, because we share many interests and hobbies. She regularly overextends herself to help others; a good nurse has healing hands and a huge heart, but a great nurse has hustle!

Pam exemplifies greatness as she scuttled to help patients, and both avert and resolve crises. After forty years of nursing, Pam recalls donning her running shoes and the required navy blue or green-only scrubs she wore daily. At the start of her shift, with seemingly boundless energy, Pam double-knots her shoes because there would be no time to re-tie, not even on a bathroom break.

In 1983, her maternal grandparents purchased a nature-blessed homestead near the Nantahala National Forest in Otto, NC. The sprawling haven has rolling green mounds, a year-round waterfall, and the sounds of birds and wildlife scurrying about leaves and a creek. A year later, her family built a large, comfortable home at the end of a long, tree-lined driveway where the entire family could gather.

Pam relaxes just thinking about her family's mountain home. She is more relaxed there than anywhere else. Upon arrival, Pam immediately goes to lie on the porch in the sunshine and doze. After unpacking, she finds herself drawn back to the sun-drenched porch to read a book or just lie there. She enjoys the solace of nature, no car noises or hospital machines beeping. While there, Pam always feels like she is in a languid state where she does not have to do something STAT! When it is time to depart, she never wants to leave but always feels restored and ready to face her world.

Years passed, Pam retired, and the home's ownership transferred within the family. Pam and her husband eventually inherited the home from her mother. As engaged parents and actively involved grandparents, Pam and Roger renovated the home for comfort and to meet their family's needs.

As a nurse, Pam knew accessibility was an important feature to create. They remodeled the home with a no-barrier doorway for safety, and chose kid, pet, and elderly-friendly furniture and surfaces. The home's vibe bounces between spaces for family fun and cozy respite. Guests do not have to worry about using the wrong towels or marring the cupboards, countertops, or floors. The whole estate is absolutely welcoming to family and visiting friends. It is dog friendly and grandbaby safe. Now they affectionately refer to their generational mountain home as "The Center of the Universe." Life there revolves with a predictable ease for the entire family.

After a busy week of caring for grandkids, cooking for family, letting a senior grand dog out for a midday comfort break, working out, and volunteering, Pam's thoughts turn to their mountain home. In the thick of caring for others, Pam shares she wants to go where "it's mine, and simple."

At the mountain home, Pam gives herself permission to pace herself, to seek restorative rest, and to pray about her struggles. In her black and tan woven cane chair on the porch, Pam rocks and sometimes has a good cry.

"I'm not really alive if I can't cry. I'm not a machine, I feel!" she expresses.

From the chair, she sometimes moves to the outdoor sofa with cushions and quickly falls asleep to the sounds of the waterfall. The porch is Pam's favorite place to have her coffee— the first cup black and alone, and the second cup is made sweeter with cream and the company of her husband.

On this same porch, her granddaughter with cerebral palsy confided to her, "I just want to be able to run like my brother across the grass, Grandma!"

A year later from the same comforting porch, Pam watches her granddaughter run, in her own way, across the grass with her brother and cousins. Along with resting, healing and growth happen here. Pam watches her grandchildren run on the grassy mounds and collect rocks from the mouth of the waterfall until darkness falls and hungry bellies need filling.

After a lifetime of running hard and taking care of people, Pam desires to be fully present with the people she loves. When exhaustion nips at her heels and she needs to rest and reset, her thoughts return to the comfort of her mountain home. She kisses Roger good night in their urban condominium already wanting to be in their mountain home. She drifts off to sleep almost smelling the laurel trees and hearing the waterfall's soul-filling melody. Sitting on her sun-filled porch or simply thinking about being there has become Pam's resetting therapy. At her mountain home, people who need love, care, attention, or respite come to her. No more running shoes are needed, but she is always up for a little hiking.

Poem
Family
Supportive, homey
Rocking, welcoming, relaxing,
Always the same home
Love

Mantra
"Love"

Pam's personal mantra is the word love. By quietly revisiting her mantra whenever she needs a moment of calm, Pam can cultivate a sense of grounding.

CHAPTER 3
Breathe In, Let Go

Every breath is an invitation to balance, release, and begin again. Take a deep breath and let go; welcome to yoga. With this wellness practice, every inhale brings you closer to balance and every exhale releases what no longer serves you. Yoga, a holistic wellness practice originating in ancient India, encompasses physical postures, breath control, meditation, and guiding principles to achieve harmony of one's mind, body, and spirit. The practice of yoga dates back thousands of years, evolving through various traditions, writings, interpretations, and trends. Yoga became popular in the western world in the Twentieth Century, and today people of all ages and abilities practice yoga worldwide to attain, maintain, and enhance their well-being. Yoga practice serves to unite the mind, body, and spirit. As a mindfulness practice, yoga helps connect us just as we are to the present moment without judgment.

As a yogi practitioner since 2007, I attained multiple certifications and serve as a teacher and continuing education provider. But most importantly, I have a personal practice. I use yoga regularly as a self-care holistic wellness practice. During Humble Warrior wellness retreats, I introduce yoga and provide participants with basic yoga equipment—a mat, a strap, and blocks. Most importantly, my nonprofit provides a certified yoga teacher to provide quality instruction for a safe, trauma-sensitive practice. Our yoga teachers are passionate and extremely well trained to lead breath-aligned movement. If you want to explore yoga, I recommend having your doctor's approval and taking an initial class with a certified yoga teacher. Yoga provides an opportunity to do something good for yourself and in turn others.

A mindful yoga practice can cultivate enhanced wellness. Mary Beth, a U.S. Air Force combat veteran and Humble

Warrior yoga teacher and board member, memorized the posture sequence from her first yoga class.

She shared, "My mind finds solace in my body instinctively knowing what to do next. Knowing the flow sequence with my eyes closed really helps me to dial in and focus on my breath."

The mantra, or catch word, she repeats to herself is, "Brave . . . I am brave." She feels brave to face whatever challenge is ahead. Mary Beth uses her yoga practice to come back from and to process challenging times and situations.

Caught in a deep reflection, she shared, "When I am in a stressful place, my breath is the first thing to go. I will constantly need to yawn or catch my breath really seeking the full, deep inhale. My yoga practice is a chance to focus on nothing but my breath and getting that deep, in the belly breath. I walk away feeling more focused and calmer."

Yoga is more than a group fitness class, workout, or twisting yourself into a pretzel. In fact, the physical practice, or asana, was designed to fatigue the body and calm the mind in preparation for meditation. The actual yoga postures, more commonly called poses, are just a small part of the larger practice that includes philosophy, ethics, breathwork, and meditation (See Appendix A – The Eight Limbs of Yoga Overview).

Claire, a former ambulance driver, proud firefighter wife, Ignite Yoga Studio owner, and Humble Warrior yoga teacher shares, "Yoga is so much more than the asana itself. I really dove deep into that understanding during times when I couldn't physically practice the postures. I tip my hat to Patanjali Maharishi and the people who put pen to paper about the ancient history of yoga. There is a deep respect in the yoga community for carrying those lessons on and off the mat."

Yoga guides practitioners towards self-awareness, inner peace, and ultimately union.

Cheri, a small business owner and Humble Warrior yoga teacher, shares,

> "I became a yoga teacher because I believe yoga philosophies can make people's lives so much better. If one practices the discipline of yoga, they will experience

less stress, less anxiety, better health, and live in harmony with others and the planet that sustains us. While practicing yoga, we bring ourselves into the current moment and practice being mindful. This allows us to let go of what is going on in the outside world. We notice what we hear, feel, see, smell, and taste without judgment. By deepening our breath and practicing different breathing exercises, we notice our breath. We release tension, stop holding our breath, and allow the energy in our body to flow freely while the body gets a break from the stress and tension our own mind puts on us."

Humble Warrior uses yoga as a valuable tool to dial down the noise of the world for our clients who serve. On duty, they are taught and conditioned to always be aware and prepared. This hypervigilance can take a negative toll on their nervous system and overall well-being. When off duty, yoga is a resource, and breath is their tool guiding them to a more relaxed state.

Reasons for Practicing Yoga

You can practice yoga for a variety of reasons. Your reason to practice may change depending on your environment, available time, or season of life. A regular yoga practice can enhance mind and body fitness, cultivate self-control and awareness, and deepen relaxation.

Here are common reasons for practicing yoga:

- ➢ **To practice self-care**: Yoga provides an integrated holistic approach to wellness.

- ➢ **To foster mindfulness and presence**: Yoga encourages being present in the moment and aware of your thoughts, emotions, and surroundings without judgment.

- **To support fitness:** A regular yoga practice can improve flexibility, mobility, strength, balance, and stability.

- **To improve proprioception**: Yoga helps improve coordination and cultivates the awareness of your body position.

- **To connect with others**: Participating in group yoga classes can foster a sense of community and belonging.

- **To practice introspection and self-reflection**: Yoga allows you to explore your inner self and deepen your sense of self.

- **To cultivate growth:** Yoga emphasizes the process of doing the practice and letting go of attached outcomes. By consistently practicing yoga, you can develop the beneficial qualities of discipline, dedication, and enhanced well-being.

- **To reduce stress:** Yoga uses breathing and relaxation techniques to calm the nervous system and promote a sense of inner peace (Woodyard 2011).

Yoga's multifaceted nature can positively impact many aspects of your life. Cheri explored yoga after suffering with restless leg syndrome for years. She experienced uncomfortable leg spasms whether sitting on her couch or lying in bed.

She recalled, "Many times I had to get up and walk around because I didn't know what else to do. I couldn't sleep! To my dismay, I was told by my doctor to take ibuprofen. 'Forever?' I inquired. Unfortunately, that was all he had to offer me. Surprise, surprise, after attending yoga class once a week regularly, I relieved my leg issue and slept more soundly. Just once a week, 'No drugs. No doctor.'"

Types of Yoga

Yoga is not one size fits all. Yoga is easily customized and blended to meet people's abilities and specific needs. There are many types of yoga making it available to a wide audience of people (See Appendix B - Types of Yoga). Personally, I like to describe yoga as being on a continuum. On one side is meditation comprised of minimal movement and breathing exercises; in the middle is hatha yoga comprised of traditional physical poses and breathing techniques; and the other side is vinyasa yoga comprised of a dynamic fast-paced flow of poses synchronized to the breath.

Humble Warrior uses gentle yoga with a trauma-sensitive approach when introducing veterans and first responders to yoga. Gentle yoga is a slow-moving practice of yoga typically suitable for all-levels, beginners to seasoned practitioners. It focuses on unhurried, gentle movements, stretching, and breathing techniques to improve flexibility, balance, and to cultivate relaxation without putting undue stress on the body. A trauma-sensitive approach is an adapted style of teaching with an emphasis on creating a safe and supportive environment for individuals who have experienced trauma. This style of yoga lands well with the veteran and first responder communities who regularly deal with traumatic events and experiences. The teaching cues emphasize mindful movement, body awareness, and empowerment without triggering or re-traumatizing participants. The yoga teacher typically offers choices, avoids physical adjustments, and fosters a sense of agency and self-regulation.

For Mary Beth, trauma-sensitive instruction came naturally. She expressed, "I wanted to create a space where someone can come and just breathe. The poses are extra. I can hold space for my community to inhale and exhale deeply."

Similarly, Claire explored trauma-sensitive yoga teaching because of things her husband went through personally and while firefighting.

Claire shared, "I know yoga can help folks. I love providing choices and options while teaching the first responder community; it works! Yoga is part of many positive things happening for the first responders regarding mental health. The stigma of trauma is being blasted, and I am forever thankful."

Yoga can be for everyone. Experienced yoga teachers have the skills to create environments and classes accessible to all people and all body types. There is great diversity within the various types of yoga. The yoga styles all coexist together and truly offer a practice for everybody! What type of practice catches your interest?

Benefits of Yoga

Yoga offers a multitude of benefits for the mind, body, and spirit fostering holistic well-being. Through breathwork, movement, and meditation, yoga integrates these elements to create a balanced and centered state of well-being.

> ➢ **Mind**: Mentally, yoga can improve focus, clarity, and emotional resilience, helping to reduce anxiety and cultivate inner peace. By providing a space for self-discovery, yoga allows you to explore your thoughts and emotions without judgment leading to greater self-awareness and emotional processing.
>
> Cheri commented, "Yoga is an amazing tool, the more I practice, the more I feel the lingering peace and calm it cultivates. I encourage people to develop a yoga practice, so when you need it in times of stress or anxiety, it can be your tool to dial down."
>
> I too believe yoga is dose dependent. My favorite pose for mental clarity is *easy pose*—simply sitting cross legged on a folded blanket. As I sit, I work to lengthen my spine and sit taller, to deepen and slow my breath, and to close my eyes or soften my gaze. When these three things come together, my thought traffic slows. As I sit longer, I feel more present in the moment and feel more at ease in my body. As the seated pose

becomes more comfortable, I feel present and grounded. For me, this pose cannot be rushed or perfected. I remind myself on days when *easy pose* does not feel so easy, yoga is a practice, my practice to do.

I quietly say to myself, "I'm right where I need to be, and I'm doing the work that is mine to do." This self-talk reminder allows me to stay and sit in the pose uncomfortably comfortable.

- **Body**: Physically, yoga can enhance flexibility, strength, and balance while promoting relaxation and stress relief. Yoga also supports injury prevention and enhanced mobility. I regularly share with yoga students that yoga makes them better at other physical activities in their lives: gardening, running, walking, and even sleeping. My favorite yoga pose for physical well-being is *tree pose*. In this alternate leg balancing pose, my stabilizing muscles activate, my stance is strong, and the noise of the world fades. Even if I fall out of the pose or wobble making it a quivering tree, I rest knowing that I can achieve balance.

- **Spirit:** Spiritually, yoga can cultivate mindfulness and a deeper connection to oneself, supporting a sense of harmony and purpose. Through introspection and contemplation, you can explore your values, beliefs, and purpose in life. Yoga can provide you with a sacred space to foster a deeper sense of spiritual connection.

Claire explains, "In your practice, you can develop the art of noticing and practicing nonjudgment. There is no guilt or shame. It is a sweet, simple, yet profound first step to just notice and acknowledge. The entire time I have been leading folks in yoga, I have had the ability to still be a yoga student and continue to learn and grow. I hope that never stops."

My favorite pose for spiritual nourishment is *savasana* pose, commonly called *corpse* pose. While lying on my back, I can just be. I have total freedom to be a human being and not a human *doing*. I enjoy the intentional stillness, the solid support of my mat on the floor, and the feeling of connection to my breath and God.

I quietly give God thanks and express gratitude for being able bodied—truly a gift I do not take for granted as a combat soldier and cancer survivor. If my body feels achy or the space is cold, I add yoga blocks under my knees, a blanket under my head, and another blanket over my body for comfort and warmth. I also enjoy using an eye pillow, a masked-shaped pouch made of soft fabric, commonly filled with rice or herbs. This additional prop provides slight pressure on my eyes and optic nerve, inducing deeper relaxation. On a personal note, my favorite eye pillow is made from a disco-looking fabric. It is filled with rice, infused with eucalyptus essential oil, and handmade with loving kindness by my cousins, Wanda and Vickie. Both are self-proclaimed military brats. Whether I hold the pose for a few breaths or several minutes in deep relaxation, I come out of the pose feeling more refreshed and grateful.

From evidence-based research to inspiring personal experiences, yoga offers a myriad of powerful benefits. Consistent practice is the key to unlocking these positive effects.

Experiencing "The Shift"

With my well-worn yoga mat slung over my left shoulder, I walked through our front door feeling refreshed. I dropped my rolled-up, organic, black rubber mat in the hall corner for easy pick up the next day. Even though I was inside, I kept wearing my comfortable blue fleece beanie because I did not have hair on my head or anywhere on my body after multiple rounds of chemotherapy.

"Too damn cold for my bald head!" I declared as I readjusted my hat.

Walking towards me, my husband Dave asked, "How was yoga class?"

Pausing long enough for him to hug and kiss me softly, I shared, "Good, I didn't think about cancer for a solid hour."

The mental hiatus I experienced in class was a healing reprieve, and the physical practice was amazingly restorative. After I was diagnosed with the "C" word, cancer became the first thing I thought about when I awoke, consumed my thoughts all day, and was always the last thing on my mind when I went to bed.

Yes, I went to bed, but I struggled to fall asleep. My sleep was intermittent as I found it challenging to dial down my thoughts. The cancer journey catch phrase "new normal" was an uninvited guest in my head. It was new, and I sure as hell did not want it to be my normal; nothing felt normal. Is this all going to be permanent? My new normal thought traffic felt like Atlanta's twelve-lane outer loop highway during rush hour—busy, full of dangers, and chaotic.

However, after yoga, and subsequently learning and practicing other holistic wellness modalities, my thought traffic resembled a meandering deer trail—calm, quiet, and familiar. I started looking forward to this relaxing shift during my group yoga classes and personal meditation practices at home. The more I engaged in these wellness practices, the faster and more often I felt the shift. For me, yoga is truly dose dependent—the more I practice, the more I experience feelings of peace and ease.

Later, I came to learn that this was a physical shift in my nervous system from the sympathetic nervous system to the parasympathetic nervous system. During yoga, my nervous system shifted from fight and flight to rest and digest.

I knew I needed to live in a more relaxed state and surge into a heightened arousal state when needed. My military experience trained me to be alert, to stay alive, to see something and say something, and to live in a hypervigilant mode. My cancer diagnosis unnerved me, and I felt like the physically fit and agile body that I relied on so heavily in service was betraying me.

I was thankful to return to my yoga practice. My medical team considered my yoga practice as complementary care in my cancer treatment. I considered prayer, plant-based eating, journaling, yoga, and meditation as primary care and chemotherapy as a complementary treatment.

I was grateful I did not have to resort to prescription pills or other forms of self-medication to dial down from my ruminating and runaway thoughts. The shift I was regularly experiencing was a key reason I enrolled in a 200-YTT yoga teacher training certification program during my cancer treatment.

After years of teaching and completing an advanced-level 500-YTT certification, additional trauma-sensitive yoga training, and living as a cancer survivor for almost a decade, I am blessed to teach yoga to the greater community and be a part an incredible nonprofit team of yoga teachers. We are honored to provide no-cost yoga classes, workshops, and wellness retreats to women veterans and women first responders for these self-care benefits:

- ✓ To calm and clear their minds
- ✓ To strengthen, lengthen, and create ease in their bodies
- ✓ To connect and create community by practicing together
- ✓ To practice self-control
- ✓ To cultivate enhanced self-awareness
- ✓ To connect their mind, body, and spirit
- ✓ To reset the nervous systems from stress.

How to Practice Yoga at Home

Exploring yoga in the privacy of your home can be a comfortable, convenient, and rewarding way to grow and integrate your own personal practice. You can weave wellness into your everyday routine right at home!

Here is a step-by-step guide:

- ➤ **Set up your space:** Find a place with enough room to move comfortably. Use a yoga mat or a non-slip surface for safety.

- ➤ **Choose your practice**: Decide on the type of yoga you want to explore. There are plenty of options to suit your needs and preferences.

- ➤ **Follow online classes or videos**: There are countless resources available online, ranging from free to subscription-based platforms offering guided yoga classes. Choose a video that matches your skill level and desired intensity.

- ➤ **Warm up**: Start with gentle warm-up movements to prepare your body for the practice. This could include simple joint rotations, stretches, and deep breathing exercises.

- ➤ **Practice the yoga poses:** Follow along with the yoga teacher, focusing on proper alignment and breathing throughout each pose. Modify poses as needed to suit your body and ability.

- ➤ **Mindfulness and breathing:** Pay attention to your breath and try to synchronize it with your movements. A good rule of thumb is to inhale as your body expands and exhale as it contracts. Staying present and mindful throughout the practice can be challenging for newcomers as well as experienced practitioners. Allow yourself to let go of any thought distractions.

- ➤ **Cool down and relax:** Finish your practice with a few minutes of relaxation or meditation. A common relaxation pose is *savasana* or *corpse* pose, which involves lying comfortably on your back while breathing deeply and following a guided meditation or systematic relaxation process.

- ➢ **Stay consistent:** Try to establish regular yoga personal practice. Will your practice be daily or weekly? You decide. Choice is empowering! We all begin our yoga journey right where we are. Consistency is the key to experiencing the full benefits of yoga.

  Even a few poses lasting a few minutes a day can bring life-changing benefits. Explore sneaking a little yoga into daily life with these tips:

  - Before you get out of bed, hug your knees for a 30 second *knees to chest* pose as you take a few deep belly breaths.
  - While sitting in a chair, enjoy the flexion and extension of your spine in a *seated cat* and *cow* pose.
  - If you find yourself standing in line, hold a *mountain* pose to enhance your stability and improve your posture.

- ➢ **Give yourself grace:** Sometimes there are too many barriers to a home practice. Other people's routines, not enough space or privacy, and distractions are just a few common barriers to having a home-based yoga practice. In this case, consider trying yoga at a studio or a community center.

  Find a location that feels comfortable, inclusive, and supports your schedule. A good rule of thumb is to try each class and instructor three times. The teacher may be having an off day or trying something new, or you may be having an off day. If you do not feel the right chemistry, try another location or teacher. After all, it is your personal practice!

Yoga is a cathartic and spiritual practice for Claire. She smiled and shared, "Sometimes there is nothing to say and nothing to be done other than holding space and breathing together."

By embracing a self-reflective, yoga practice at home or in a studio, you can experience enhanced well-being.

Breathing Practices

Breathing practices are techniques that focus on controlling and manipulating the breath. They can be stand-alone practices and are often integrated as complementary practices in yoga. Mary Beth's favorite way to teach a yoga class is to hold each pose for two to three breaths minimum.

She explains, "This allows the person to focus on the feeling of the pose in their body, and how to breathe through something that may be a bit uncomfortable."

While teaching, Mary Beth often cues when to inhale and exhale as a reminder to both take and release that deep breath. Breathwork is beneficial for your well-being due to its ability to regulate the autonomic nervous system, reduce stress, enhance mental clarity, and promote relaxation. Most yoga practices encourage breathing in and out of your nose. The nose filters, warms, and moistens your breath.

Claire equates pranayama, or breathwork, as a simple tool; she shares,

> "The easiest way to apply, or live, yoga off the mat is to use the very breath itself. Our breath is a tool in our personal toolbox. We carry our breath tool everywhere and into every situation. By intentionally stopping what we are doing to take a breath in and a breath out while thinking about nothing else, we can stimulate our vagus nerve. This nerve carries signals between our brain, heart, and digestive system, and resets our own nervous system.

> An extended exhale makes me think about my son's heart condition. His cardiologist described to me the vagus nerve tentacles wrap around the atrioventricular node when it is stimulated. And that is when the reset of the heart happens. The node acts as a gatekeeper, regulating the timing of these signals to ensure the heart beats in a coordinated and efficient manner. There is breathwork for everything! I'm thankful my young boy has this breath tool to activate his vagus nerve in his own personal toolbox when needed."

Breathing exercises can also work to improve respiratory function, increase oxygenation of the blood, and boost immune function. Here are two examples of breathing practices:

- **Belly Breathing:** This technique is also known as diaphragmatic breathing and involves breathing deeply into the diaphragm rather than shallowly into the chest. When practicing belly breathing, the belly expands on the inhalation, then the chest cavity expands. On the exhalation, the chest softens, then the belly. To connect with your breath easier, you can place your left hand on your belly and your right hand over on your chest as you breathe. Engaging the diaphragm promotes relaxation and reduces the activation of the sympathetic nervous system, specifically the fight or flight response (Ma, et al. 2017).

- **Alternate Nostril Breathing:** This technique involves inhaling and exhaling through alternate nostrils while using a hand technique to regulate nostril airflow. Studies have shown that after a five-day practice of alternate nostril breathing, the practice effectively reduces hypertension (Kalaivani 2019).

To practice this technique simply follow these steps:

1. Sit comfortably and lengthen your spine.
2. Allow your left hand to rest on your lap.
3. Use your right thumb to gently close your right nostril.
4. Inhale slowly through your left nostril.
5. Close your left nostril with your right ring finger, release your thumb, and exhale through the right nostril.
6. Inhale through the right nostril.
7. Close the right nostril, release the left, and exhale through the left nostril.
8. Repeat for three to five rounds, breathing smoothly and calmly.
9. Return to your normal, unrestricted breathing for three breaths.
10. Repeat the sequence, beginning with the left nostril closed.

There is a wide and diverse range of breathing practices, and each has its own aim to enhance well-being. As a yoga teacher, I like to share in my yoga classes, "Hold the pose, but not your breath. If you lose the pose, but keep the breath, that is still good yoga."

Your Yoga Invitation

Your yoga practice can be a few mindful breaths daily, a traditional class in a studio, or something in between. Know that yoga does not require us to practice it perfectly. In yoga there is no perfection; there is only practice. A personal yoga practice provides the opportunity to yoke our mind and body to achieve harmony. You are invited to incorporate a yoga practice and breathwork into your life for positive change and long-lasting wellness benefits.

Yoga and Breathwork Reflection Questions:

1. Which specific yoga or breathwork exercises did you find helpful? Why?

2. How did your perception of yoga change after reading this chapter?

Image courtesy of Humble Warrior Wellness & Yoga

You could explore and incorporate these four yoga poses—bridge pose, reclined spinal twist, knees to chest, and legs up the wall—into your bedtime routine for relaxation.

Spine Movements

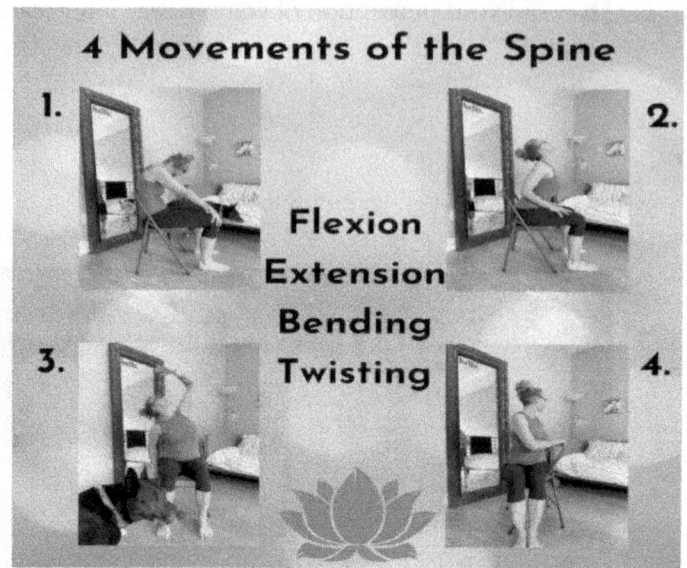

Image courtesy of Humble Warrior Wellness & Yoga

You are invited to explore these four yoga poses—cat, cow, crescent, and seated spinal twist—for a refreshing stretch, especially if you sit for extended periods.

JAMES'S STORYBOARD
The Porch

Chaos	Dangerous Patrol Officer Job
Anchor	Front Porch
Calm	Personal Mantra of "Refuge"

"Shots fired! Homicide in Two Rivers."

I'd been on solo patrol for a year, and the weight of the situation hit me immediately. Two K9 officers arrived on scene first, but the suspect was nowhere in sight. The next radio call was for reinforcements. We needed a solid perimeter. I joined two other officers to secure the area. As we worked the perimeter, every action was deliberate. At one point, we had to assist each other over a wobbly and worn fence with our shields and rifles in hand. Our adrenaline was running high when we spotted a man sitting in a car parked in the driveway. He became our focus. Approaching cautiously, I ordered him to put his hands up. Instead, he feigned sleep. The tension grew, and my teammate yelled at him to put his hands up. He ignored the intense and clear command and reached between the seats instead. Our team moved decisively, and we got him out of the car. A follow-up search revealed a handgun wedged between the front car seats.

Meanwhile, SWAT was thoroughly briefed and deployed to the known flop house where the victim's body was found. It was a common practice for people to flee out of the back of flop houses. Once SWAT arrived, they systematically cleared the house and detained everyone inside. The house was buzzing with activity. Adding to the chaos, an unknown car circled the block repeatedly and stopped behind the house. The occupants were watching the scene unfold. We kept our eyes on both the house and the suspicious car.

By then, resources from three major departments were on-site working together. The overlapping call signs and commands created radio chaos. I was in the thick of an active homicide investigation, and relied heavily on my training, the direction of senior officers, and the support of my teammates. It was intense; there is no other word for it. But the day wasn't over. A tip came in, and once again, resources were rallied and redeployed. The car we'd been monitoring had picked up people who had fled the house earlier and taken them to a location in Manitowoc. We set up another perimeter, and SWAT detained the suspects without incident.

Later, detectives from multiple agencies pieced together the story. A young man had been shot and killed after a petty argument. The 21-year-old suspect had pulled a gun to act tough but ended up taking a life. What stayed with me wasn't just the intensity of the day or the massive coordination of resources, it was the total lack of remorse from the suspects. They didn't care. It was apathy, the complete disregard for human life. Bad things happen, and bad people exist. It's why we do this job. On that day, we did it twice.

####

I first met James at his police academy graduation. We stayed in contact, and I came to understand the intensity of his rookie years.

James's parents always had a nice house. From his cradle to his college years, they provided him with a highly personalized room and stylish home where he could live and thrive. Yet as a first-time homeowner, James bought a big, ugly, yellow house and describes his home as "hard on the outside, and soft on the inside."

One look at James in his police uniform and you could draw the same conclusion. A tall, muscular build and piercing blue eyes create his hard exterior, but not at all ugly nor yellow in spirit. The curve of his mouth when he smiles hints at a boyish charm and provides a peek at a caring and softer inside. His house is not guest ready. Everything is slightly askew. He must clean up or clear off something before unlocking and opening his raspy front door.

Almost everything James has is a hand-me-down, donation, or a re-gifted item from a friend or family member. He does not need new things; the items he has acquired have continued purpose. The article's origins are known and comforting like a favorite pair of worn jeans. His parents gave him familiar and lovingly worn furniture. The upright piano and accompanying faded floral-patterned covered bench were a gift from his aunt and uncle who live nearby. The only art in his living room is a gift from a college friend, a mesmerizing heavy wooden, geometric mosaic. She knew James would never buy art in a store. The two friends still exchange handwritten letters; relationships matter. The rocking chair James positioned to face the front door belonged to his grandparents. Everything about James's home is worn but not tattered. It is a lived-in kind of home. While possessions are not his priority, James thinks of his circle of friends and family in each of their donated items now decorating his house.

Being at home is comfortable. James boasts that he can fall asleep anywhere, but the easiest is in his home. He would rather get up early to arrive somewhere and sleep in his own house than elsewhere to get a few more winks.

"I sleep well because it's secure, no unexpected visitors, curtains are closed, bushes block a direct view, and the door windows are high and very private."

Every time he is sleeping, James holds and hugs something. He self-admits, "I like cuddles, dammit!"

When sleeping in his own home, he does not worry about what other people are doing. Sleep comes easily, but it is not deep. He will wake up if he hears something. If someone walks through his house, James can tell what room they are in by the sound his home makes. The center board in the living room squeaks, the whole stairway whines, and the corner leg of his bed groans against the hardwoods. It is like a customized security system. Daily, the scent of cinnamon-infused coffee lingers heavily on the main floor. He knows his guests can almost taste the scent, but strong coffee fuels James for his third shift patrol work and his responsibilities as a sergeant.

The one aspect of James's home life that helps him dial down from work is his porch ritual. James's porch-sitting is the culminating reward of a healthy control ritual. His routine is always the same, and it brings him comfort. On warm days, he mows the lawn. Chaotic weeds and unruly grass become a meticulous mat with patterned lines. He eats dinner, a hamburger, and then sits on an outdoor rocking chair donated from a work friend. He is grateful the chair rocks so he can slightly recline and lean back.

With a refreshing stretch, James shared, "Leaning back means I'm not working on a call or writing a report."

After the sweaty satisfying work of cutting grass and eating dinner, he holds a cigar in one hand and grabs a cold Hamm's beer in the other. Then, he sits. He hits shuffle on his favorite playlist and immediately alternative upbeat songs fill his manicured refuge. The sun shines on to the freshly cut lawn through the rooftop and the limbs of the large Maple tree in the front yard.

James sits far enough off the road so he can watch people without people watching him. It is a day he can control, unlike at work where there is no controlling the events of his shift. James is fulfilling his calling to serve and protect his community. While wearing the badge number of a fallen colleague, James works earnestly, tackling tough jobs and training to rise through the ranks. By adding credentials in drug recognition and accident review, and serving as a ballistic shield instructor, a K9 decoy, and on the warrant service team, James ensures his community and circle of friends and family is safer. Service drives his purpose! On his porch, James allows in the feeling of relaxation. He feels filled, satisfied, and secure. His Dad laughingly calls porch sitting barking at cars.

When James stays awake to be a part of family events, outings with friends, and monotonous work moments, he knows his comforting home awaits his arrival. Pulling up to his house and seeing his inviting porch gives him an instant feeling of tranquility. When James has been awake for twenty-four hours on patrol, he turns inward, reflecting on the times he spends on his porch to reset and refresh his focus.

Being at home is comfortable, secure, and safe. Sitting on his front porch is a reminder that he has control, can relax, and be present in the moment. James embraces the quiet, resetting time on his porch. Occasionally, he barks at a car and knows somewhere his dad is too!

Poem
Porch
Secure, comfortable
Reclining, watching, being
Patterned lines of grass
Refuge

Mantra
"Refuge"

James's personal mantra is the word refuge. By quietly revisiting his mantra whenever he needs a moment of calm, James can cultivate a sense of grounding.

CHAPTER 4
Nature's Reset Button

"May your life be like a wildflower, growing freely in the beauty and joy of each day."
– Native American Proverb

Nature has the power to reset, restore, and rejuvenate. By fostering a deeper connection with nature, you can explore a holistic approach to wellness that nurtures the mind, body, and spirit. Engaging in outdoor activities is vital for personal well-being. Mother Nature is an incredible nurturer!

It is no coincidence that we seek her loving care when we desire a mood, perspective, or energy-level change. Our innate appreciation for her abloom leads us to seek vacations at the beach and mountains, gaze at sunrises and sunsets, and enjoy immersive flora and fauna experiences. Whether connecting with nature in your backyard, a community park, or another location, you can weave nature-centric activities into your wellness routine. This chapter explores the key aspects of restoration, reasons for engaging with nature, the benefits of being more outdoorsy, and highlights easy-to-do outdoor wellness activities.

Reasons for Taking Your Life Outdoors

During the COVID-19 pandemic, my nonprofit saw a growing demand for wellness workshops, classes, and services. To ensure safety while maintaining connection, we moved our programs outdoors. In the open air, we could safely distance yet foster meaningful connections. We also discovered that nature itself offered the powerful benefit of tranquil restoration. The calming influence of natural environments promoted a deep relaxation, a sense of ease, and feelings of joy. Conversations lingered longer as people embraced a shared sense of calm and comfortable togetherness. Today, there are many compelling and evidence-based reasons to incorporate outdoor activities into a wellness routine.

Here are some of the key reasons to connect with the outdoors:

> ➢ **Grounding**: Engaging in outdoor activities can promote a deep sense of tranquility and restore overall well-being. Emerging research and advocates of barefoot practices and earth-friendly products highlight the benefits of physically connecting with the Earth's surface. This act of grounding, or earthing, involves reconnecting the body to the Earth's natural electric charge through direct contact with the ground (Ober 2010).
>
> Your body is conductive. By simply placing your hands, feet, or body in direct contact with the earth, you can experience this restorative process. Common grounding practices include standing or walking barefoot on grass, sand, or soil, lying directly on the ground, or wading into natural waters.
>
> Personally, I find the beach to be an ideal setting for grounding. There, I exchange the busyness of life for peaceful sunrises and ditch my shoes for bare feet. It reminds me of the laid-back vibe of country music singer Zac Brown Band's song "Toes" with its lyrics describing putting your toes in the water and sitting in the sand, capturing the essence of total relaxation.
>
> ➢ **Air quality:** Outdoor environments generally offer fresher and cleaner air compared to indoor settings. Indoor air pollution can arise from household chemicals, mold, and inadequate ventilation, contributing to respiratory stress and illness.

Conversely, outdoor air, particularly in nature settings, tends to be less contaminated with pollutants and richer in oxygen. I intentionally select pristine beaches, lakes, and mountain locations for wellness retreats to harness the positive effects of fresher air, salty breezes, and radiant sunshine.

Humble Warrior alumnus and U.S. Air Force veteran Tammy shares, "Nature has taught me to slow down and look around. I am more engaged, more curious, and less anxious when I am outdoors."

➢ **Unplug:** The modern reliance on digital screens can lead to several adverse effects including eye strain, disrupted sleep, and increased stress. In contrast, viewing natural scenes has been associated with reduced stress, improved mood, and enhanced cognitive function. One study found that individuals who spent time looking at natural images reported lower stress levels and greater psychological well-being (Jo, et al. 2019). An outdoor wellness practice allows us to regularly ditch our screens.

Tammy attests, "With my phone muted or safely stowed, I stay engaged in outdoor activities longer than indoor activities because I feel a part of something much larger. There is a world out there and when I am in it, I am part of it! The more time I spend outdoors, the more I appreciate the world in which we live."

➢ **Vitamin D:** Exposure to sunlight is a primary source of Vitamin D, an essential nutrient for bone health and immune function. Vitamin D deficiency can increase susceptibility to infections, disease, and illness. Sunlight exposure facilitates the production of Vitamin D in the skin, supporting our immune system. Since you can receive more Vitamin D from sunshine than food sources, I make it a year-round personal practice to get a minimum of twenty minutes of sunshine without any sunscreen. If I stay longer, I am diligent about using mineral-based sunscreen protection.

> ➤ **Nature Deficit Disorder**: Richard Louv, in his book *Last Child in the Woods*, coined this term to describe the growing disconnect between children and nature. While not a diagnostic medical term, it is a metaphor for what he sees as the impact of this separation on mental and physical health. Children now suffer from reduced attention spans, reduced concentration, reduced creativity, increased moodiness, anxiety, short-tempers, and obesity. Louv provides research showing the lack of outdoor time has a negative impact on mental health and well-being (Louv 2005).

Benefits of Outdoor Activities

By channeling your inner naturalist, you can improve and support your overall well-being. The outdoors is available to us like a constant companion.

There are many benefits of fostering a deeper connection with nature:

> ➤ **Improved Emotional Stability:** Engaging with nature supports overall mental health. Schoolchildren and teachers equally appreciate a refreshing recess break. Likewise, Humble Warrior solidified the practice of including immersion in nature at our in-person events. I consider it a one-size-fits-all holistic medicine. In nature, people get the dose they need whether energy, relaxation, or calmness. One study concluded that a mere hour of contact with the earth improved mood more than expected by relaxation alone (Chevalier 2015).

➢ **Enhanced Physicality**: For many people, activities like hiking, gardening, and birdwatching can become more than just hobbies; they turn into grounding wellness practices. By moving your birdwatching from a quiet indoor pursuit to the outdoors, you can shift from passive observing to active engagement. By increasing your physical activity, birdwatching becomes following the chirps and calls, finding nests, or even setting up feeders to invite nature closer.

For me, the more I immerse myself, the more comfortable I feel stepping outside, even on a rainy day. Last summer, I was thrilled to see the brown pelican, a nonnative species and huge bird, make its way to the shores of Lake Michigan in my hometown of Manitowoc, Wisconsin. I was so excited that I took my dog, Grace, for a walk past Blue Rail Beach and all the way to the Breakwater Lighthouse just to check out the sighting and snap a few pictures. We even made a stop at the city dog park on the pier, which was a win for both of us! Outdoor activities not only boost cardiovascular fitness but also a sense of peace and connection with the world.

➢ **Increased Mindfulness:** Being in nature encourages awareness, which can reduce stress and improve emotional regulation. Nature exposure can also foster a deeper connection to the environment and support a greater sense of calm. Many meditation recordings and apps focus on the sounds of nature. Calm, a top-rated app for sleep, meditation, and relaxation uses water, breeze, and bird song to stress less, sleep more, and live mindfully (Calm 2012).

➢ **Boosted Immune System**: Exposure to natural environments can enhance immune function. Dr. Qing Li, a physician and immunologist specializing in environmental medicine and the health benefits of forest bathing, explored the role of phytoncides, airborne substances released by plants and trees that can boost our body's natural defenses. Phytoncides increased the activity of people's natural killer cells that target harmful cells (Li 2010).

As a cancer survivor, I learned that spending time in nature could help increase my natural killer cell activity, which plays a role in fighting off illness. I might not fully understand the science, but I knew I wanted my immune system in fighting shape and loved the idea of having my own army of natural killer cells. To support my own immunity, I started taking leisurely daily walks on a nearby nature trail with my older dog, Radar. We enjoyed soaking up the fresh air and new scents while I boosted my immune system. Over time, these walks became a healing ritual for both my battled body and spirit.

➢ **Supports Better Sleep**: Natural light exposure helps regulate sleep patterns and improve sleep quality. In Dr. Li's work on forest bathing and environmental science, he highlights how exposure to natural elements like sunlight helps the body's circadian rhythm, or sleep-wake cycle. Natural light helps regulate people's energy, signaling when to be alert and when to rest (Li 2018) This helps us feel more awake and energetic during daylight hours and promotes restful sleep as night falls.

➢ **Strengthens Social Connections:** Participating in group activities outside fosters social interaction and community building. Group hikes, community gardening, beach clean-ups, and outdoor yoga classes are all ways to connect with others while being in nature. Being outside together allows us to bond over shared experiences, such as planting a community garden or finding wild berries on a hike. These interactions not only deepen our relationships but also enhance our collective well-being.

How to Cultivate an Outdoor Practice

Outdoor enthusiasts naturally gravitate toward spending time in nature, needing no extra encouragement to get outside. But if you are someone who needs a little nudge to step outdoors, that is perfectly okay. I am not a fan of tent camping, humidity, or spiders—especially after a brown recluse spider bite. Even so, I routinely spend time outside with my family, our dogs, and by myself. I help people cultivate a greater appreciation for nature by inviting them to join me in nature-centric activities, from hiking to air shows.

You can begin by exploring the outdoors in small doses. Our nonprofit believes in the power of outdoor experiences and incorporates them into wellness programs, offering something for everyone. Whether it is sitting, reading, journaling, or walking, many people find peace and restoration in being outside. For those seeking more active pursuits, we explore outdoor yoga, gentle and challenge-by-choice hiking, boat rides, paddle boarding, and kayaking. When Tammy spends time outdoors, she chooses activities that have both physical and mental attributes.

"I am a have my cake and eat it too kind of person" describes Tammy.

Her favorite outdoor activity du jour is kayaking. She says, "du jour" because she always enjoys rotating among a variety of outdoorsy activities like camping, hiking, and trail running.

Tammy explains, "With kayaking, I can easily have both the physical and mental component. Flatwater paddles afford me the opportunity to physically exercise my body, but the serene environment offers plenty of opportunity to meditate, reflect, and be aware of my co-existence with nature. Moving water, or whitewater, pushes me physically. It also gives me an opportunity for mental conditioning, goal setting, and confidence-building."

Whether you want to savor stillness and solitude or explore your deep connectedness with one another, here are some economical and accessible practices to help you connect with the outdoors:

➢ **Forest Bathing:** Shinrin Yoku, a Japanese wellness practice of immersing oneself in a forest environment, has gained global recognition for its numerous health benefits such as lowering blood pressure, reducing stress hormones, and enhancing immune function (Li 2018).

Despite its name, forest bathing does not involve taking a bath; rather, it is a mindful practice of simply being present in nature, whether walking slowly or sitting quietly in a forest setting.

Here are a few simple steps for practicing forest bathing:

- o Find a quiet natural setting: Choose a forest, park, or natural area where you can disconnect from distractions.
- o Leave technology behind: Turn off your phone and other devices to fully immerse yourself in the experience.
- o Engage your senses: Notice the feeling of the air on your skin, the rustling of leaves, and both the scents and sounds of nature.
- o Walk slowly and explore stillness: Wander without a destination in mind, noticing sights, sounds, and scents. Savor moving slowly and mindfully. Pause periodically to sit or stand quietly, allowing yourself to fully absorb the peace of the natural surroundings…simply notice what you notice.

➢ **Walking**: Walking or gentle hiking is an intentional form of movement. Whether in a local park, nature reserve, or along a nearby trail, walking offers numerous physical and mental benefits. With minimal equipment, just comfortable shoes and weather-appropriate clothing, you can walk at a relaxed pace for leisure, recreation, or exercise.

Many embrace walking as a wellness practice for both physical stimulation and mental calm. Walking in a natural setting enhances grounding and fosters a sense of self-acceptance.

Mary Beth feels a sense of deep connection as she walks in the woods, "Good, bad, or indifferent, I feel like the space has a vibration. It's as if I can feel the energy of the place but only if I'm not distracted with my phone or something else." When she is immersed in the present moment, Mary Beth adds, "I feel connected to something larger than myself. It's a connection to nature, to the real world, not the digitally constructed one."

By paying attention to what she can hear, see, smell, touch, and even taste, Mary Beth leaves the forest feeling grounded and connected, more herself than when she started. Many find earbuds playing music, podcasts, or audio books keep them moving on runs, hikes, and jogs. While these are great for the cardiovascular system, they lose some of the benefits of mindfulness. On occasion, try a quiet walk.

➢ **Gardening**: Cultivating plants can be a fulfilling and restorative practice, whether done in a backyard, a porch, a community garden, or on a windowsill. This activity not only enhances mood and reduces stress but also offers the reward of growing your own vegetables, herbs, flowers, or plants, fostering a deeper connection to nature.

In a reflective moment, Tammy shares, "I grow with my garden. Gardening is not always easy and the old me would say I have failed a million times. In truth, I haven't failed at all. Each new gardening season has been an opportunity to learn from every seed as it grows, blossoms, or lays dormant. My garden has taught me that I, too, am not perfect, and that is beautiful. While my favorite moments in the garden are the first leaves pushing up through the dirt and the first blossom on a tomato plant, I am most grateful for the spent plants that are withered and composted. They assure me that a new season will again happen, and we can continue to grow together."

Even a small garden affords the opportunity to interconnect with the larger ecosystem. Your flowers are pollinated by a myriad of insects that also feed the birds and other creatures. Gardening is a way to give back to nature while also creating a beautiful space filled with butterflies, bugs, and birds.

Additionally, a garden offers the joy of watching things grow. Nothing connects you to weather patterns quite so much as being invested in the survival of your trees, plants, and flowers. Some gardeners are motivated by nostalgia, striving to cultivate heritage plants once grown by their ancestors. They may want to recreate the flowers in their grandparents' yard or grow the berries and tomatoes they fondly remember from their childhood but can no longer find in supermarkets.

I was elated when my mother gave me six raspberry branch stem cuttings from her grandfather's garden for my box garden. Those sweet berries filled my belly, but more importantly, they filled my love tank.

There are people who are regulars at the gym but would never consider using those muscles to build a rock wall, dig deep holes for new trees and shrubs, push wheelbarrows full of compost, or squat and bend to plant and weed. There is physical exercise to be had in the garden.

As an additional reward, every tree planted helps to clean our air and house a multitude of critters. You might consider gardening as a way of tithing your money, time, and energy toward the stewardship of nature.

> **Birdwatching**: Birdwatching is the practice of observing and identifying various bird species in natural environments, whether in parks, gardens, or even your own backyard. This mindful activity offers a calming yet mentally engaging experience. You can opt for a more active approach, such as hiking, or guided field trips with your community's birding group.

Although you could spend thousands of dollars chasing a bird list all over the world or buying an expensive camera for the perfect bird photo, the equipment needed is minimal. A pair of binoculars and a bird guide, whether in book or app form, is enough to begin your journey.

Valerie, a Humble Warrior supporter and military family member, is an avid birder and finds it an enjoyable, low-cost, and all-seasons hobby that connects her to nature.

She shares, "Many birders get hooked because someone puts up a bird feeder and starts to get familiar with some of the regular feathered visitors. From there it is easy to learn the names of a few species. As the bird watcher's interest grows, he or she begins noticing bird behaviors like who hogs the feeder and who is a grab-and-go eater like a chickadee or titmouse who takes a single sunflower seed and flies off to crack it open somewhere else. Then, they also notice what birds stick around all year, and which birds are seasonal visitors."

With a smirk of experience on her face Valerie adds, "Those questions get carried out beyond the feeder and into the world. In any case, that is how I started. I learned a little bit and then added on to it. I am a rank amateur in the birding world."

Valerie admires people who can identify birds by identifying one among thousands of songs and calls, but she is content as a novice. Learning new things about nature and observing birds in their natural habitats enhances Valerie's connection to nature.

She expresses in appreciation, "A little bit of knowledge increases my awareness of the world around me and enhances my regular walks in the woods where I live. I grin at the call of a pileated woodpecker, enjoy that brilliant flash of color of an indigo bunting, and sometimes get a bit ruffled myself when I scare up a ruffed grouse along a rail-trail path. It brings a feeling of familiarity and emphasizes to me how connected everything is in fitting into their environmental niches."

For Valerie, birding is just one part of her nature-centric wellness routine. She becomes wonderfully immersed in all the different lichens, mosses, fungi, and ferns during her walks in the woods. To counter "warbler neck" from binocular use and the aches from prolonged standing as she distinguishes a raven from a crow, Valerie also incorporates a few discreet yoga poses. For her, birding is a regular practice of immersive and restorative moments in nature.

While all these activities offer many benefits, activities in nature have inherent risks because Mother Nature designed the outdoors, not engineers and lawyers. Please use caution outdoors and be aware of your surroundings for your personal safety. I have been stung by bees, bitten by a spider, wiped out on an ocean wave, and admittedly felt lost in the woods a time or two. But I still explore and engage outside regularly. There truly is something for everyone to safely discover, explore, and enjoy in nature.

Your Outdoor Invitation

Nature-centric activities provide countless benefits for personal wellness from cleaner air and reduced stress to stronger immunity and improved mental clarity. The stark difference between natural and artificial environments highlights the necessity of weaving nature into our daily lives. By making outdoor activities and direct engagement with nature a priority, you can profoundly enhance your overall well-being. Like most mothers, Mother Nature truly knows best and nurtures our entire being. Whether forest bathing, walking, gardening, birding, or discovering another activity, she is waiting to greet you. How will you connect with her as part of your wellness journey?

Nature Immersion Reflection Questions:

1. What is your relationship with nature, and how does it influence your sense of calm?

2. Think of a time when nature helped you reset or find clarity. Could this be a grounding anchor for you?

MARSHA'S STORYBOARD:
The Waterfalls

Chaos	International Military Crisis
Anchor	Waterfalls
Calm	Personal Mantra of "Calmness"

We were circling the Persian Gulf when an unexpected event happened. Our ship, an aircraft carrier powered by eight nuclear reactors, suddenly went down to just two reactors online. As an engineer, I was standing watch in the fore plant. When the reactors scrambled, I followed the procedure. I immediately began taking emergency measures: reducing power, communicating to the bridge exactly what was happening, and shutting throttles as needed. I also coordinated with my reactor operators to reduce more power to stabilize all systems.

We were already operating under abnormal conditions, with four of the reactors cross-tied. We conducted calorimetric tests, a method to measure and calibrate the reactors' control system. At the same time, a small training drill was underway in the aft group, where the back four reactors are located. When one aft reactor went offline during the drill, the other three reactors followed. Reactors are essential to an aircraft carrier—they provide propulsion, power, and electricity. While we had emergency backup diesel generators, they were not meant for the full demand of our carrier's systems. In that moment, everything depended on our training, teamwork, and focus. We took well-rehearsed immediate actions. Those first emergency actions only took a few minutes to render a safe condition. However, it would take several hours to recover fully and bring everything back online.

It was harrowing because an aircraft carrier's main defense is its jets. With only two reactors online, we could not launch any jets. An emergency call went out to our battle group—about 20 ships and submarines soon surrounded us. These ships shielded us while we worked to get the reactors back online. It was the first time I ever saw the rest of the fleet. What made it even more nerve-wracking was the presence of Iranian forces. We did not know it at the time, but they attempted to encroach the one-mile radius of our ship. Our massive battle group pushed the Iranians back.

That day serves as a powerful reminder of how quickly cascading failures can spiral, but it also showcased incredible teamwork. We worked together under pressure to stabilize the situation and bring the ship back to full operational capacity. Despite the fear and intensity, I still feel a deep sense of pride in what we accomplished on my last deployment in the Navy.

# # # #

Marsha attended one of my wellness retreats during Covid and has remained very active in our nonprofit. She made an effort to intentionally connect to our wellness mission. One of her many activities with us is leading book club discussions.

Always swallowed up with highly technical work requiring isolation, resilience, and vigilant monitoring both in her US Navy and civilian life, Marsha actively seeks adventure and community outdoors. As a self-proclaimed explorer, she maintains a ready backpack full of "what-if" stuff. Her kit, as veterans affectionately call the backpack, includes a compass, emergency blanket, spare socks, first aid supplies, medication, raingear, and a canine rescue wearable sport sack.

By adding snacks and drinks for herself and Chakotay, her trail experienced sheltie-mixed canine, the kit is adventure ready! Years ago, Marsha rescued this sickly litter runt from a woman in a Walmart parking lot. She named him Chakotay after the First Officer and first Native American main character in the Star Trek franchise. With no known tribal affiliation for either the character or dog, Marsha embraced Chakotay as family, honoring her own Muscogee ancestry.

On a spring day, Marsha clasped the waist and chest straps of her hefty, lavender-colored kit around her sturdy five-foot frame.

Chakotay, now fully grown, completely deaf, and half-blind, stood leashed and ready at her side. These often-misjudged companions set off for a new destination adventure at Desoto Falls. Brimming with excitement, Marsha was ready to explore the falls—two distinct cascades surrounded by lush greenery. They linked up with a group of women Marsha met on Facebook. The ad hoc hiking group completed the short, quiet, uneventful hike quickly. It wasn't the immersive, serene escape Marsha had hoped for all week.

A random woman from the group piped up suggesting they grab some food at JR's Roadkill BBQ and hike nearby Helton Creek Falls—a captivating natural wonder also nestled within the Chattahoochee National Forest. Marsha had blocked the entire day for adventure and considered the invitation. Seeing the patio seating was dog-friendly and there was plenty of daylight, Marsha stayed with the group.

After a friendly lunch, the six women and Chakotay hiked single file and comfortably close to one another. They passed through fragrant mountain laurels and rhododendrons as they traversed the root-tangled and narrow path. Upon reaching the charming pair of waterfalls, the group spread out taking in the magnificent upper falls' sixty-foot drop. Equally impressive were the lower falls which cascaded over a thirty-foot ledge, releasing into a natural swimming hole at its base. The unequal pair of waterfalls appealed to Marsha. She easily released her full attention to the picturesque rock formations and liquid ambiance. The gentle pool of North Georgia water was clear, no murkiness.

Marsha pondered about the E. coli levels and then released those busy thoughts to Mother Nature. They entered the pool, and the rocky bottom proved slippery on bare feet and paws alike, so Marsha kept Chakotay tethered closely. She secretly wishes Chakotay could hear the droplets bounce up and down at the base of the frothy falls. Ice cold mountain creeks fed the falls. The sunbaked rocks and mossy covered shadows were an intense contrast to their frigid flow. The sensory experience of swimming in that space, this pool of swirling water and sparkling sunshine, consumed her awareness.

With skin tingling, Marsha shares, "When my work hits an overload tipping point, I hike to the falls. I have been there four or five times. It is relaxing to just think and talk about it."

Her favorite season is spring, but Marsha's waterfall is accessible to her in any season of weather. By simply turning inward, Marsha has learned she can mentally return to the laurel-laden path, cascading falls, and a feeling of serenity as an effective wellness practice.

Poem
Waterfalls
Beautiful, slippery
Hiking, listening, swimming
Smell of mountain laurels
Calmness

Mantra
"Calmness"

Marsha's personal mantra is the word calmness. By quietly revisiting her mantra whenever she needs a moment of calm, Marsha can cultivate a sense of grounding.

CHAPTER 5
Eating for Energy and Clarity

What we eat directly impacts how we feel, think, and move through the world. Do certain foods or drinks make you feel energized, comforted, sleepy, or improve your concentration? Of course they do! Our intake fuels and affects our wellness. If you have ever woken up groggy, felt a midday slump, or eaten dessert for dinner, welcome to being a perfectly imperfect human being.

By exploring a whole food and plant-based diet filled with nutrient-rich foods like fruits, vegetables, whole grains, legumes, nuts, seeds, and spices, you can support your overall well-being. Additionally, proper hydration supports bodily and cognitive functions to reduce stress while promoting relaxation, calm, and balance. Hydration is closely connected to good nutrition.

There's No Perfect Diet!

A healthy diet can help stabilize blood sugar levels, provide essential nutrients, and promote beneficial gut flora. But, how do you know what to eat? There is no one perfect nutritional diet because individual needs vary based on factors such as genetics, age, gender, activity level, medical conditions, and environmental factors. Additionally, cultural preferences, family traditions, and economic factors influence dietary choices.

Although not found in his writings, the ancient wisdom of "let food be thy medicine and medicine be thy food," is attributed to the famous Greek Physician Hippocrates. He makes the connection that food can heal and prevent disease. By subscribing to this mindset, you can use the Humble Warrior simplified rule of thumb that whatever you eat or drink is either helping or hurting your wellness.

The Plant-Based Diet, the Mediterranean Diet, and the Traditional Japanese Diet prioritize whole, nutrient-rich foods and are associated with positive health benefits. However, individual customization may be important to meet specific nutritional needs. Research studies provide evidence supporting health benefits associated with each of these diets.

Let's look at some of the healthier ways of eating in the world:

- **Plant-Based Diet**: This diet is centered around fruits, vegetables, nuts, seeds, legumes, and whole grains. It is linked to lower rates of obesity, heart disease, high blood pressure, and certain types of cancer (Greger 2015).

- **Mediterranean Diet**: This diet is rich in fruits, vegetables, whole grains, fish, nuts, and olive oil. It is associated with numerous benefits, including reduced risk of heart disease, stroke, and certain types of cancer (Sofi, et al. 2008).

- **Traditional Japanese Diet**: This diet emphasizing fish, seafood, tofu, vegetables, rice, and green tea is low in saturated fats and high in antioxidants and omega-3 fatty acids. It is connected to lower rates of mortality, disability, and dementia (Matsuyama 2022).

However, there is an increasing reliance on fillers, substitutes, and genetically modified organisms (GMO) in most of our foods. GMO food-like substances are foreign to our bodies. Additionally, pesticides, forever chemicals, and toxins are appearing in our foods and bodies. The introduction of pollutants into the world's oceans is overwhelming its natural filter and cleaning processes. Common contaminants found in our oceans include heavy metals such as mercury and lead, and persistent pollutants, pesticides, and microplastics.

More than one-third of the shellfish-growing waters of the United States are adversely affected by coastal pollution (National Oceanic and Atmospheric Administration 2024).

The Food and Drug Administration and the Environmental Protection Agency co-published an *Advice About Eating Fish* chart. The chart's intended use is to help people choose which fish to eat and how often to eat them based on their mercury level, a neurotoxin that bioaccumulates in fish. If it is important for you to eat real food, take comfort in knowing the above three diets prioritize whole, nutrient-rich, and primarily plant-based foods (Food and Drug Administration & Environmental Protection Agency 2021).

My Food Transition Story

So, why do I follow and promote whole food and plant-based eating? Aside from my health, the short answer is ahimsa, a Sanskrit word meaning nonviolence. Ahimsa supports the concept of compassion or doing no harm. Years ago I was introduced to the word as a key cornerstone in my two-hundred-hour Yoga Teacher Training. The concept of compassion for self, others, and our shared world was woven into the entire curriculum. A requirement for the course was agreeing to follow a plant-based or vegan diet.

I was already leaning toward a plant-based diet after my son, Tyler, and I watched the documentary *Forks Over Knives* (Fulkerson 2011) Tyler recommended the movie after watching it in one of his high school classes. The movie follows a fire station making the plant-based diet shift and provides supporting facts and research. Tyler and I immediately cleared out a lot of our family's pantry. We cooked lentils, quinoa, and brown rice to support a variety of vegetable toppings and zesty sauces.

To support our yoga class's dietary change, the class cooked and ate together, used recipes from a common cookbook, recorded our intake on a daily wellness chart, and used litmus paper to measure the amount of acidity or alkalinity in our urine. Additionally, we read and discussed well-documented, evidence-based books supporting the many benefits of following a whole food and plant-based diet.

During my yoga certification course, I was in active treatment for advanced-stage cancer and wholeheartedly welcomed the whole food and plant-based benefits of reduced inflammation, nutrient absorption, and better gut health.

After several chemotherapy treatments, my oncologist told me I was "sailing through treatment."

I thought to myself, "no one sails through cancer treatment," but the comment reinforced my adherence to a strict whole food and plant-based diet. I was having so much success that I hired a private nutrition team specializing in supporting oncology patients as complementary care. My nutrition team, comprised of one PhD in Nutrition and one MD, confirmed that the plant-based diet lacked Vitamin B12, so I began taking a weekly sublingual supplement. My team tracked my labs, provided nutritional guidance, and worked to identify and cut off the cancer's pathway with nutrition and supplements. Our joint goal was to help ensure my chemotherapy treatment was as effective as possible while minimizing the negative side effects.

From my yoga course, I purchased the following four books, three evidence-based books and one cookbook, for my personal library and as go-to references for my healing journey: *How Not to Die* by Michael Greger, MD with Gene Stone, *Anticancer: A New Way of Life* by David Servan-Schreiber, MD, PhD, *Healthy at 100* by John Robbins, and the cookbook *Oh She Glows* by Angela Liddon.

Additionally, our yoga course involved watching vegan documentaries as a class and assigned homework involving family and friends. My motivation to follow a whole food and plant-based diet was highly personal . . . I wanted to survive, to live!

However, after watching shocking stories of animal agriculture practices, the marketing industry's manipulation, the deplorable treatment of animals, and vast clearing of land to feed agricultural animals, my motivation to stay on a plant-based diet expanded to support animal welfare and environmental sustainability.

An ahimsa diet involves doing the least amount of harm to humans and other beings. By eating a whole food and plant-based diet, you can garner positive health benefits and support both animal welfare and environmental sustainability. My big takeaway from this dietary transition is that what you choose to consume affects not only you, but also our environment, and agricultural animals.

Embracing a "More" Plant-based Plate

My nonprofit teaches and explores incorporating more plant-based diet programs, because we embrace evidence-based and trauma-sensitive wellness practices. A whole food and plant-based diet is supported by quality research and embraces compassion, and it meets our criteria of evidence-based and trauma sensitivity. Additionally, I regularly share fun food facts I learned from earning my Holistic Nutrition certificate and from my own healing journey experience. In our programs, we share information about the pH spectrum, the importance of eating the rainbow, tips on how to become more plant-based, and our favorite recipes.

The pH Spectrum: Acid to Alkaline

The pH spectrum is a measurement tool identifying the acidity or alkalinity in a substance. For our use, foods are categorized as acidic, neutral, or alkaline based on the pH level. The pH scale ranges from 0 to 14, with 7 being neutral. Below 7 is considered acidic and above 7 is considered alkaline.

Consuming a variety of foods is important to digestion, the absorption of nutrients, and the reduction of inflammation.

> ➢ **Digestion:** The body has a mechanism for regulating pH levels, the stomach. G. J. Tortora and B. Derrickson, authors of the *Principles of Anatomy and Physiology*, explain how the stomach plays a crucial role in digestion by secreting gastric acid, primarily

hydrochloric acid (HCl), which helps break down food and kill bacteria (Tortora, et al. 2017). The stomach's pH level is highly acidic and ranges from 1.5 to 3.5. This acidity is necessary for optimal digestion and the activation of digestive enzymes.

➢ **Absorbing Nutrients:** Tortora and Derrickson go on to explain how the pH of the digestive environment also affects nutrient absorption. Different nutrients absorb optimally at varying pH levels. For example, calcium absorption occurs better in a more alkaline environment.

➢ **Inflammation:** Plant foods are typically alkaline-centric, and they support the reduction of inflammation. At our wellness retreats, the idea of reducing inflammation is universally appealing to veterans and first responders.

Many participants are dealing with ruddy complexions, irritated skin, achy joints, migraines, and fighting or surviving cancer, so we highlight increasing the consumption of alkaline foods—fruits and vegetables. Dr. Michael Greger, a renowned physician and author of the best-selling book How Not to Die, discusses the benefits of a plant-based diet for reducing inflammation and promoting overall health (Greger 2015). He emphasizes the importance of consuming a wide variety of fruits, vegetables, whole grains, legumes, nuts, and seeds which are rich in antioxidants, phytonutrients, and fiber.

The impact of food pH on digestion, nutrient absorption, and inflammation varies among individuals and may be influenced by other factors such as overall diet, health status, and digestive or medical conditions. Consulting your physician is always advised as you consider changes in your nutritional intake.

Eat the Rainbow!

Different colored foods often contain various nutrients and phytochemicals beneficial for good health. A simplified rule of thumb is to "eat the rainbow." Eating the rainbow translates to consuming a diverse array of colorful fruits and vegetables and is generally recommended as part of a balanced diet to ensure a wide range of essential nutrients and health-promoting compounds (Massey Cancer Center 2018).

Here is a straightforward and simplified explanation of how different colored foods can contribute to your wellness:

- **Green Foods:** Green vegetables like broccoli, kale, and spinach are rich in chlorophyll, fiber, vitamins (including vitamin K and folate), and minerals (including potassium and magnesium). At our wellness retreats, we present that these green foods support the detoxification processes due to their high content of antioxidants and phytochemicals.

- **Red Foods:** Red fruits and vegetables like tomatoes, red berries, and red bell peppers are high in antioxidants (including lycopene and anthocyanins). These red foods support your heart and cardiovascular processes.

- **Yellow and Orange Foods:** Yellow and orange fruits and vegetables like sweet potatoes, carrots, and oranges are rich in vitamin C, beta-carotene, and antioxidants. These yellow and orange foods support body functions: vision, skin, and joints.

- **Purple and Blue Foods:** Purple and blue fruits and vegetables like eggplant, blueberries, and purple cabbage contain anthocyanins and antioxidants. These purple and blue foods support longevity.

Consuming a variety of fruits and vegetables helps ensure a diverse intake of vitamins and minerals to enhance your wellbeing. I like to think the pot of gold, at the end of my eating my rainbow, is enhanced wellness!

What About Protein?

A commonly asked question about not eating meat is, "Will I get enough protein?"

According to the American Dietetic Association, "It is the position of the American Dietetic Association that appropriately planned vegetarian diets, including total vegetarian or vegan diets, are healthful, nutritionally adequate, and may provide health benefits in the prevention and treatment of certain diseases. Well-planned vegetarian diets are appropriate for individuals during all stages of the life cycle, including pregnancy, lactation, infancy, childhood, and adolescence, and for athletes" (Craig, et al. 2009).

Some sources of protein to explore include the following: legumes (beans, lentils, and chickpeas), tofu, tempeh, seitan, nuts (almonds and walnuts), seeds (pumpkin and sesame), whole grains, and dark leafy greens (spinach and kale).

Additionally, research indicates, "Consuming foods rich in Vitamin C alongside iron-rich foods can enhance iron absorption" (Hunt 2003).

Tips on How to Become More Plant-based

People eat the foods they eat for a multitude of reasons ranging from comfort, stress-level, economic-level, tradition, to status and convenience. Changing eating habits requires effort. From my collective experience, I noticed most people did not make significant and enduring changes until they, or a loved one, had a medical crisis or scare. I have received numerous calls from nonprofit alumni, their loved ones, family and friends—often after a diagnosis of disease or condition. Then, there is always a sense of urgency in transitioning to a more plant-based lifestyle. I am always quick to share that I am not a clinician, but I am happy to share what I have learned from my personal experience and holistic nutrition certification.

After my diagnosis, my doctor did not recommend a specific diet. Instead, I was simply advised to eat enough to ensure I got sufficient calories. The nutrition information from the medical facility was a few handouts and the highlight was the American Cancer Society's website.

Ugh! I learned about the positive impact nutrition and supplements could have from a relative who was in cancer remission. What she shared built upon the information that I learned in my yoga teacher training and encouraged me to willingly pay to use the same nutritional team she used.

My nutrition team shared, "If we do not get what need from our diets, we will draw what we need from our bones, organs, and skin."

In short, we will become depleted. I truly do not want you to have to experience a diagnosis, disease, or injury to explore the benefits of a more plant-based diet. These tips can help you adopt a more whole food and plant-based diet.

Start slowly and know that small steps can lead to gradual and enduring changes. Ten strategies to help achieve change are listed below:

1. Focus on whole foods by limiting or avoiding processed foods, sugary beverages, and trans-fat.
2. Eat less dairy and meat products.
3. Add a large salad topped with zesty spices daily.
4. Meal swap by substituting a plant-based ingredient in your favorite meal (i.e., beans or tofu for hamburger).
5. Practice Meatless Monday by going meatless for an entire day.
6. If you choose to consume alcohol, do so in moderation and consider dry red wine, cold-filtered beer, and high-quality tequila. These may be easier for the body to process.
7. Become a flexitarian by eating a "mostly" whole food and plant-based diet.

8. Watch evidence-based documentaries such as *Forks Over Knives* and *What the Health.*
9. Experiment with new recipes to find out what you really enjoy and to prevent boredom.
10. Be prepared by keeping a well-stocked kitchen pantry with plant-based staples to make it easier to prepare nutritious meals. Ingredients like legumes, grains, and a variety of fruits and vegetables can be used in many plant-based dishes (Turner-McGrievy, et al. 2015).

Tips on Encouraging Others to Become More Plant-based

If you live with your family or have roommates, involve them in eating a more whole food and plant-based diet! Having the support and assistance of family members can make this transition a fun and lasting experience.

Wanting to reap the benefits of whole food and plant-based eating, Jess, a Humble Warrior alum, began meal prepping and eating more fruits, vegetables, and seeds. Soon after, her family's nutritional mindset and habits changed.

Her daughter Erika shares, "I remember Mom incorporating healthier options for me. If I wanted a snack, she would always add some fruits or veggies. Instead of going to McDonald's, we'd go to a sit-down café to eat. Not only did I think that it emotionally brought us more together, it also broadened my horizon for different types of food. There are still a lot of foods I won't eat, but now that I've tried different foods groups, I know there's a lot more I'm willing to eat."

Explore These Seven Family-Friendly Food Tips:

- ➢ **Lead by Example:** Role model plant-based eating behaviors. Let your children see you enjoying fresh, whole food. I like to call it "get caught crunching!"

- ➢ **Involve Your Family in Meal Planning:** You can teach, demonstrate, and of course sample your creations to foster a positive food environment!

- **Make it Fun:** Experiment with themed meal nights and grow some vegetables in a windowsill planter, outdoor pot, or garden! Share plant-based corny jokes! How does a cucumber become a pickle? It goes through a jarring experience.

- **Gradual Transition:** Go slow to create lasting change. Your family may need time to adjust to new flavors, textures, and smells. Consider introducing new foods in a variety of recipes and conditions. In my own family, my husband loves raw carrots but does not like them steamed or roasted.

- **Shop Smart:** Whole food and plant-based shopping can be more affordable when you purchase seasonal produce, bulk staples, and utilize frozen or canned items. Use discernment to ensure your food is whole or minimally processed and looks fresh. Fancy packaging and convenience size can increase food costs.

- **Be Patient and Supportive:** Allow your family to make personal choices and encourage learning more about whole food and plant-based eating together.

- **Learn Together:** Explore Dr Greger's *Daily Dozen* app. This is an easy to use and free app highlighting what and how much you need to eat daily.[13] Additionally, I encourage you to read annually the *Clean Fifteen List*, fruits and vegetables with very low traces of pesticides, and its sidekick, the *Dirty Dozen List*, fruits and vegetables with high traces of pesticide residues published by ewg.org (Environmental Working Group 2024).

Sample Plant-based Menu

Seek specific guidance from a nutritionist or your physician to plan your meals to provide a balance of carbohydrates, protein, healthy fats, fiber, vitamins, and minerals essential for supporting your desired energy level and physical activity. Adjust portion sizes based on your individual calorie needs.

Here is a sample menu for you to explore.

Breakfast: Smoothie Bowl

Ingredients: Mixed berries (strawberries, blueberries, raspberries), banana, spinach or kale, and almond milk or coconut water.

Toppings: Sliced almonds, chia seeds, shredded coconut, and (homemade) granola.

Directions: Blend berries, banana, spinach or kale, and almond milk or coconut water until smooth. Pour into a bowl and top with sliced almonds, chia seeds, shredded coconut, and granola.

Lunch: Quinoa Salad with Chickpeas

Salad Ingredients: Cooked quinoa, chickpeas (drained and rinsed), cherry tomatoes (halved), cucumber (diced), red onion (chopped and rinsed), fresh parsley (chopped).

Dressing Ingredients: Lemon juice, olive oil, mustard (Dijon or your favorite), garlic, salt, and pepper. Whisk the ingredients well.

Directions: In a large bowl, combine the cooked quinoa, chickpeas, cherry tomatoes, cucumber, red onion, and parsley. Drizzle and then toss with lemon dressing.

Dinner: Vegetable and Tofu Stir-Fry

Ingredients: Firm tofu (pressed and cubed), mixture of vegetables (broccoli, carrots, snap peas, and peppers), garlic (minced), ginger (grated), low-sodium soy sauce or tamari sauce, sesame oil, and brown rice.

Directions: In a large skillet or wok, heat sesame oil over medium heat. Add garlic and ginger and cook until fragrant. Add tofu and cook until golden brown. Add mixed vegetables and continue to stir-fry until fork tender. Add soy or tamari sauce and cook and stir for a minute. Serve over brown rice.

Sometimes it is nice to have a delicious meal, both hot and cold, so I am excited to share my Quinoa Harvest recipe. It is my go-to tasty, alkaline meal! My daughter-in-law Maddie loves it cold, and I can't resist it when it's hot; it's perfect either way! Gather fresh ingredients, assemble them with care, and enjoy the simple pleasure of creating a nourishing meal. Whether you savor it warm or chilled, this dish is sure to become a staple in your kitchen. Pick up what you need today and experience the vibrant flavors of this wholesome recipe.

Quinoa Harvest Recipe

Ingredients:
- *1 – Jar of palm hearts*
- *4 – Cobs of fresh sweet corn or frozen baby corn (uncooked)*
- *1 – Pint of cherry-type tomatoes*
- *1 – Juice of lemon*
- *2 – Cups Cooked Quinoa*
- *1 – Cup Baby Kale or Spinach*
- *Avocado (optional)*

Directions:
Cut palm hearts into ½" segments (small circles).
Cut corn off the cob or open and thaw frozen baby corn.
Cook Quinoa with kale or spinach (shredded leaves, no stalks).
according to the quinoa directions.
Cube the avocado into bite sizes.
Combine all ingredients in a large bowl.
Squeeze lemon juice over the top and mix well.

Note: You can enjoy this hot or cold. Try eating it as a meal or scooping it on top of a green mixed salad.

Your Rainbow Eating Invitation

You now have evidence-based reasons, useful references, helpful tips, a sample menu, and my favorite alkaline-based recipe to prioritize your own whole food and plant-based eating plan. While there is no perfect diet, a more whole food and plant-based intake coupled with proper hydration can help fuel and enhance your wellness. How will you begin to eat a rainbow of foods to enjoy a variety of nutrients in your daily life?

Eating for Energy and Clarity Reflection Questions:

1. Did the chapter inspire you to make changes in your diet? If so, how?

2. What challenges might you face when transitioning to a more whole food and plant-based way of eating, and how can you overcome them?

JESS'S STORYBOARD
The Cozy Couch

Chaos	Sensitive Crime Convictions
Anchor	Cozy Couch
Calm	Personal Mantra of "Cozy"

Chaos was a constant, heavy presence in my job as a sensitive crimes lieutenant detective. One of the hardest assignments I ever faced required me to review thousands of child pornography videos seized from a predator's computer. Each one was more horrifying than the last. My task was to choose five clips that could be used as evidence for the prosecution. These videos documented unimaginable harm done to children. The weight of these crimes was crushing. I couldn't sleep. I started questioning whether I could even keep doing this work.

That night, as the images kept replaying in my mind, I prayed: "God, if You want me to do this work, You have to help me. You have to block these images."

He did, as only God can do. I slept and woke up with a sense of peace that gave me the strength to continue fighting for victims.

# # # #

Jess joined a Humble Warrior retreat at the cusp of her retirement. Having gained successful strategies, she continues to enroll in the retreats year after year, always enhancing her wellness practices.

Jess stays busy. She pulls out her complex daily to-do list and sighs, "There's always something to do."

The intricate and highly personalized list keeps her focused and successful in life. Over the years, many of them as a single mom, a U.S. Air Force Reservist, and a full-time law enforcement officer, Jess has tailored her list to better serve her family, personal life, and work life commitments. She crafts the list by making a cross on the paper, creating four equal portions. The top left quadrant identifies her personal priorities, while the top right is reserved for work. The bottom left identifies key times such as appointments and briefings, and the bottom right is for family obligations. As a former military court reporter, she uses her own coded short-hand, meaningful ticks, and completion markings. Admittedly, if she does not accomplish the list, it causes her great stress. In turn, she is mindful to only have three tasks in each category. And, yes, this process continues for the weekends with slight modifications.

With the list in hand, Jess seeks out calmness before facing her daily to-do storm. Jess finds the calmness she seeks in the early morning when her home is clean, and her family is still asleep or awake in another room. She makes a fully leaded cup of coffee in her renovated, very efficient kitchen and jokes that her coffee can "sit on the edge of the counter without falling off because it's that strong!"

Jess clutches the fully filled ceramic Cracker Barrel coffee mug because it is the biggest one in the house and a Christmas gift from her daughter Erika. She heads into the living room to curl up on her brown leather reclining couch as the new day's sun fills the room with natural light. She sets the coffee on a sturdy wood end table, flicks the gas fireplace on, and reaches for a multi-colored and flannel-backed quilt that a high school friend handmade for her over a decade ago.

After covering herself with the quilt, and adjusting both head and footrests for optimal comfort, Jess nonverbally cues her two dogs to join her. Penny, a brindled-colored labrador mix rescue, jumps up and lands flanking Jess's right side. Jess feels Penny's heavy pressure on her legs and gently rests her hand on the dog's silky soft back. Charlie, a woolly Welsh terrier, is in the crook of Jess's left arm and his tiny body somehow sprawls across her chest. The dogs help create a welcoming zen with their low energy and weight on her body.

Jess shares, "Their job is to lay on me, provide that pressure, snuggle, and sleep. I'm always doing something or have something to do. When the dogs are on me, I do not want to disturb them. Getting up is a major production. I'm just tucked in and feel a sense of peace, and that life is good."

Jess sits for almost an hour in silence as she sips her coffee and reviews the daily to-do list.

Part of Jess feels bad that she does not want to be around people. She has always been that way. People come to her office randomly, and she does not appreciate pop-in visitors at home. She is always hospitable but secretly waits for them to leave. Alone on her cozy couch, Jess finds the calmness that fuels her for interaction in a busy and noisy world. There, she recalls from taking her sister's yoga class that it is okay to be a human being and not always a human doing. The inviting living room draws her to the couch early in the morning each day. When she travels or is gone from home for too long, she misses her morning home routine.

Even though Charlie died May 6, 2023, Jess can close her eyes and still feel his comforting rear paws on her arm and pressure on her chest. Now she nestles on her cozy, comfortable couch with just Penny. As coffee vapor rises in the air, Jess thinks about her upcoming day. She knows this stillness benefits them both. People at home, in the department, and in the community need her. During her off time, Jess enjoys the comfortable stillness that the cozy couch scene provides. This is where her nurturing happens. For Jess, the snuggled-in life is perfect!

<u>Poem</u>
Couch
Peaceful, safe
Inviting, nurturing, relaxing
Comfortable beacon of stillness
Cozy

<u>Mantra</u>
"Cozy"

Jess's personal mantra is the word cozy. By quietly revisiting her mantra whenever she needs a moment of calm, Jess can cultivate a sense of grounding.

CHAPTER 6
Journal Your Way to Peace

The simple act of writing can unlock clarity, calm, and deeper self-awareness. Journaling is an inexpensive and accessible holistic wellness practice used to attain, maintain, and enhance overall well-being. My nonprofit's definition of journaling is the self-reflective act of regularly recording your thoughts without judgment for the purpose of cultivating personal well-being. Thoughts may encompass your feelings, activities, and experiences. This chapter highlights reasons for journaling, examines the types and benefits of journaling, and provides practical tips to cultivate your own journaling practice. These aspects of journaling draw upon research, expert and experienced opinions, and personal stories.

Reasons for Journaling

You can write in journals for a variety of reasons, and they may change with the seasons of your life. Here are common reasons for journaling:

1. To practice self-expression, introspection, and self-reflection
2. To analyze your patterns and decisions
3. To increase your emotional awareness
4. To explore your experiences
5. To change your outlook
6. To practice self-care
7. To record-keep

Journaling is introduced as a stand-alone wellness modality at our wellness retreats. We teach it at our introductory retreat to ensure a collective understanding of what journaling is all about, why we do it, and how to do it. Our nonprofit was blessed to have our co-founder and former board member Teresa, a retired high school English teacher who taught journaling. She launched and led our journaling workshops for several years.

She instilled the mindset, "There is no right or wrong way to journal" which softened expectations and removed self-imposed pressure.

Teresa opened each workshop by sharing, "Writing our thoughts, feelings, and actions down in a journal allows us to craft and maintain our sense of self and solidifies our identity. Keeping a journal can give us a chance to create and consider the narrative of our lives, with all the choices that make us who we are today."

While being taught as a stand-alone wellness modality, journaling became a companion activity to other wellness practices too. By combining journaling with other wellness practices like yoga, hiking, and cooking, there was deeper introspection.

Participants recorded their retreat intentions and personal reflections after each retreat activity. They also documented favorite recipes, quotes, random sketches, and contact information of new friends. It was common to see each woman carrying and using her journal throughout the retreat.

Humble Warrior incorporates journaling into wellness retreats for these potential self-care benefits:

1. To calm and clear your mind
2. To enhance your self-awareness
3. To build your serenity
4. To identify things that go unnoticed
5. To develop an attitude of gratitude
6. To keep you accountable
7. To provide solutions

Benefits are unique to each person. Teresa reminds us, "Each of us has faced joyous occasions, losses, disappointments, and many unexpected events. How we have dealt with them has brought us to where we are today."

Teresa ends the journaling workshop by sharing her biggest takeaway, "I learned through journaling how to think about what I thought about."

In psychology terms, this is metacognition or awareness, understanding, and even control of one's own thought processes. I hope you are thinking about cultivating your own journaling practice.

Types of Journaling

Journaling encompasses a variety of types, and each style serves a unique purpose. Collectively they provide the opportunity to promote self-awareness, reflection, and personal growth. Since journaling is an open-ended wellness activity, it can be used for many purposes ranging from creative writing to goal setting and self-reflection.

Let us explore several common types of journaling and their specific purposes.

> ➤ **Gratitude Journaling:** The practice of recording what you are thankful for. It helps cultivate a positive mindset by focusing on the good in your life, which may increase happiness and reduce stress levels. Research suggests that gratitude journaling can enhance your overall well-being by promoting optimism and resilience (Emmons et al. 2003).
>
> ➤ **Reflective Journaling:** The practice of recording your thoughts, feelings, and experiences to gain personal insight and understanding. It encourages self-reflection, introspection, and personal growth by examining your beliefs, values, and behaviors. You may enhance self-awareness, critical thinking, and decision-making skills through reflective journaling.
>
> ➤ **Creative Journaling:** The practice of recording your thoughts, feelings, and experiences visually that

expands beyond traditional writing. It incorporates using various forms of expression such as sketches, doodles, photographs, mixed media, and collages allowing self-expression and fostering creativity.

➤ **Goal-Oriented Journaling**: A technique used to clarify, track, and achieve your goals. It involves setting a specific goal and then regularly reflecting on progress, obstacles, and strategies in your journal. This process may help you stay focused and more accountable, increasing the likelihood of goal attainment.

A widely used framework for setting effective goals is SMART. The acronym SMART stands for Specific, Measurable, Achievable, Relevant, and Time-bound. George T. Doran introduced the concept of SMART goals (Doran 1981). SMART goals are effective because they provide a clear framework for setting and achieving objectives. Research suggests that setting goals improves your performance and productivity across various domains, including personal development (Locke et al. 2002).

➤ **Dream Journaling:** The practice of recording your dreams in a journal immediately upon waking. The intent is to capture as many details as possible about your dreams to include emotions, sensations, symbols, or recurring themes, to gain insights, track patterns, or become aware of unresolved issues.

➤ **Travel Journaling**: The practice of recording your experiences, observations, and thoughts while traveling. It typically involves documenting notable details from destinations visited, cultural encounters, local cuisine, and memorable moments. Travelers often use mixed mediums for journaling, including digital images, apps, and collages made of travel paraphernalia such as ticket stubs, maps, and receipts. Travel journals can become tangible records of your adventures and cherished mementos.

- **Prayer Journaling:** The practice of recording your personal prayers for yourself and others. Instead of saying prayers silently or aloud, you write them in your journal like a letter to God. It can help you grow in your prayer life, reflect on God's love, and remember your prayers. You may choose to reread entries and annotate answered prayers with additional words or a special symbol.

- **List Journaling:** The practice of recording specific lists such as your habits, food, or water intake, or maintaining a log of your mood, exercise, or tasks accomplished. This list or log-style of journaling may help you attain specific goals. Examples include recording twenty minutes of outdoor activity daily to reap the sun's Vitamin D benefits and logging food daily to identify a food sensitivity.

- **Therapy Journaling:** A therapeutic tool to explore your innermost thoughts, feelings, and experiences without judgment. It is also known as journal therapy or expressive writing. You can practice this individually or as part of a formal therapy process under the guidance of a therapist with the purpose of gaining self-awareness, emotional healing, or personal growth.

These are just a few examples of the diverse types and purposes of journaling. The type of journaling you choose will depend on your preferences, goals, and intentions for personal growth, self-discovery, and wellness.

During a difficult season of life, Teresa used the Reflective Journaling style.

Teresa shared how she developed an attitude of gratitude:

"In 2009, I retired from teaching, my youngest son graduated from college, and my mother passed away. In 2011, my husband passed away after five battles with cancer. I was now an orphan, a widow, a retired teacher, and a mother of adult children. What was I to do? As a Christian, I was supposed to feel blessed and thankful that Mother and Randy were in heaven and no longer suffering. I was supposed to accept all of this as God's plan. Well, I failed! I was hurt, angry, and confused. I was ALONE!! I needed to express my teetering emotions. I needed to vent my anger, my fears, my dreams, my desires without being lectured or judged. I needed someone to talk to; no, I needed someone who understood what I was going through and who would listen. I had taught journaling to my students but hadn't tried it myself. I never had the time or the need. In 2011, I had more questions than answers. Through journaling, I was able to answer my questions and cultivated an attitude of gratitude. I wrote, and still write, my journal entries to *Daddy God* who helped me realize which thoughts, feelings, and actions that I needed to change for me to survive...and thrive. Journaling helped me understand how much God has comforted and blessed me and continues to comfort and bless me."

While journaling helped Teresa process and answer questions, she developed an attitude of gratitude from regularly doing the practice over time.

Benefits of Journaling

Incorporating journaling into your lifestyle as a wellness routine can lead to profound transformations and long-lasting benefits. We see these benefits in Teresa. She is now filled with and fueled by gratitude! Gratitude shines through in her interactions, teaching, and actions.

Journaling stands out as a powerful tool for promoting and enhancing mental, emotional, physical, and spiritual well-being and is beneficial in the treatment of Post Traumatic Stress Disorder (PTSD).

> **Mental:** By providing a space for self-reflection and self-expression, journaling allows you to explore your thoughts and emotions. It can lead to greater self-awareness and emotional processing. According to a study published in the Journal of Clinical Psychology, journaling can reduce symptoms of depression and anxiety (Pennebaker, et al. 2007).

Teresa desired more peace, love, and joy in her life. By journaling, she uncovered, "The main thing that kept me from achieving peace, love, and joy in my life was negativity. My journal entries guided my life and strengthened my faith. I now realize that while I can't control my circumstances, I am totally in control of how I deal with them."

On July 24, 2018, she sat on her deck with her journal and focused her thoughts on the peace, love, and joy she found.

Then, Teresa opened her bible and rested on the following scripture passage, John 14:27 (WEB) where Jesus says, "Peace I leave with you. My peace I give to you; not as the world gives, I give to you. Don't let your heart be troubled, neither let it be fearful."

Then she turned to John 15:9 (WEB) where Jesus charges us, "Even as the Father has loved me, I also have loved you. Remain in my love."

Jesus brings together peace, love, and joy in John 15:11(WEB) when he says, "I have spoken these things to you, that my joy may remain in you, and that your joy may be made full."

In that moment, Teresa understood that her peace, love, and joy come from Jesus and that she can lose places, people, and purpose without losing peace, love, and joy.

Her final entry was, "We are given peace and joy, and we are to give love. If I continue to give love, I will receive peace, love, and joy. My peace, love, and joy are forever!"

- **Emotional:** Regular journaling allows you to see patterns in your emotions and behaviors. This observation may lead to positive changes and the development of helpful coping mechanisms. Writing about stressful or traumatic experiences has been shown to decrease the intensity of negative emotions and improve overall psychological well-being (Smyth 1998).

  Research identified expressive writing, a form of journaling, as a beneficial tool for people with PTSD. Journaling resulted in reduced trauma symptoms and improved mood states (Frattaroli 2006).

  Gail, a Humble Warrior alumnus, was shockingly served divorce paperwork enroute to our wellness retreat. After crying for miles and a sleepless night, she found solace in the act of journaling her emotions, thoughts, and feelings. By writing these things down, Gail gained some clarity and could process her situation more clearly.

- **Physical:** Journaling may contribute to overall physical wellness and longevity by reducing stress and promoting relaxation. Research suggests that journaling can strengthen the immune system, reduce blood pressure, and improve sleep quality (Smyth, et al. 2008).

During my own battle with advanced-stage uterine cancer, I journaled regularly each morning to have a safe place to express my many fears, to log my treatments, to record my prayers, and to create a bucket list. By writing down these things, I felt freer to focus on my healing. The act of journaling became a cornerstone of my self-care plan and a welcomed reprieve.

As my healing journey progressed, I remember the moment when I journaled that cancer was not the first thing I thought about in the morning when I woke up, or the last thing I thought about before going to bed.

> **Spiritual**: Through introspection and contemplation, you can explore your values, beliefs, and purpose in life. Journaling can provide you with a sacred space to foster a deeper sense of spiritual connection. Darci, a certified fitness instructor and friend living with recurrent cancer, maintains an online gratitude journal. Daily, she posts three things she is grateful for as part of her wellness routine.
>
> At the time of this writing, Darci had made 10,839 entries, equating to almost ten years of journaling. One day's entries are: three things for which I am thankful: (10,837) fun with family, (10,838) beautiful day, (10,839) evening devotion.

From research to transformational personal stories, the benefits of journaling are powerful and many. To harness the positive benefits of journaling, ensure you practice it with regularity. You can determine whether that becomes a daily entry, a weekly summary, or an event-driven activity.

How to Journal

Let's journal! Cultivating a journaling practice can be challenging. Like any good habit, you build your skill with regular practice over time. Creating a supportive framework for your writing is important.

Begin with finding a quiet and comfortable place, preferably in your home, where you can dial down and reflect without distractions. Next, identify a specific time of day when you can write freely, alert, and unhurriedly. You can then select the type of journal you are most interested in exploring or simply use the suggested writing prompts (at the end of this chapter) to begin. If you do not have a preference, my recommendation is to use gratitude journaling. By recording three things you are grateful for on a regular basis, you can foster a positive mindset and enhance overall well-being.

Next determine how often you will write, daily, weekly, or event-driven occasions. You decide—choice is empowering! Damen, a single military dad, attended Humble Warrior's *Journaling for Military Families* workshop and decided to try gratitude journaling. Since he had joint custody of his children, Damen maintained a dedicated gratitude journal with his family. Each child listed three things for which they were grateful. Over five years later, their journal has become a treasured family memoir.

You are free to write about whatever comes to mind without judgment. Remember, there is no right or wrong way to journal. Just write!

Here are some additional tips for a successful journaling session:

1. Maintain privacy. Select a place to write in your journal that offers you privacy and is free from criticism. Likewise, store your journal in a location that is private yet convenient to retrieve regularly.
2. Choose an appropriate journal for your style. Your journal is a private place to record your reflections.

Do you prefer a book, notebook, digital device, or a digital app? For example: left-handed people may prefer a spiral-bound journal, so it lies flat when they journal.
3. Select a writing utensil for your style. Do you prefer writing with a pencil or a pen? What color ink?
4. Date your journal entries. You may find having the date and day useful when re-reading or referring to an event.
5. Be truthful. You are the only person who will read this.
6. Reread your entries periodically. You may notice patterns.
7. Give yourself time to reflect and process the experience after writing.

Are there barriers? Of course there are! Many journaling practitioners begin begrudgingly, cannot dedicate the time, or lose focus of their reason for journaling. If finding time is challenging, I encourage you to carry a small notebook in your backpack, bag, or purse to capture both meaningful and spontaneous moments. You can jot down thoughts while waiting for an appointment, a line from a book, or a reflection from a conversation with a friend. Think of jotting in your notebook as easing into journaling. While teaching people how to make a journal entry, Teresa instructed everyone to date their entry.

Immediately, one participant, Jess, a police officer, shouted, "No way! That's evidence."

We all laughed with Jess, but we fully realized it was a privacy barrier to writing freely. Writing freely is not risk-free! Even if you keep your journal in a secure location, other people, such as a roommate or a family member, may find and read it. In the event of Teresa's death, I promised her I would gather all her journals so her adult children would not read them. My husband Dave and I have her permission to read them (or not) while sipping on a bourbon at a campfire and then burning them all!

Another barrier is the blank page. Some people just stare and cannot imagine how to start. In this case, writing prompts are extremely helpful. In your journal, with plenty of time, grace, and gentleness, explore a variety of writing prompts.

I encourage you to try these ten writing prompts over the next ten days to cultivate or jumpstart your journaling practice.

1. For whom in your life are you most grateful?
2. Where did you see beauty today?
3. When do you feel most energized?
4. Why are you living in your current home?
5. How do you feel about celebrating birthdays?
6. What was your best moment this year?
7. What is your favorite book?
8. What is your favorite tradition?
9. What season of the year are you most grateful for?
10. What is the most recent thing you have learned?

A Personal Wellness Practice

Some people take to journaling quickly. By embracing self-reflective practice, they can experience enhanced well-being. Let us look at Amy's well-established journaling practice. Amy, a Humble Warrior supporter, begins each morning with a quiet, devotion time.

"I listen to hear what God is leading me to pray for each day and write out my prayer in a prayer journal."

Her journal entry is usually a few lines, but the last sentence always reads the same.

She writes, "Holy Spirit, guide my life and give me joy. In Jesus's name I pray. Amen."

Her constant listening and seeking guidance in its purest sense, she explains, is being in a perpetual state of prayer. She knows the bible instructs followers to "pray without ceasing," which is what Amy strives for, but she admits, "I am not quite there yet."

Additionally, Amy keeps a prayer list in a separate journal with specific requests. As she prays over the list, she draws a circle around the request when it has been answered or resolved.

She beams, "There are a lot of circles!"

Prayer continues throughout her day. As she walks into her office, she often prays for those on the other side of the door. She asks God, "Lead me to lead well." Amy's work, filled with dynamic personalities and drama, is the source of her greatest challenges.

She believes, "This is an invitation to bring Jesus into my workspace. In my journal and throughout my day, I ask God to use me, and bring me more compassion, patience, and confidence as I interact."

Through prayer journaling, Amy has recognized the ability she calls "to listen past the hurt." She adds, "I absolutely know this is only possible with God's help because my human eyes only see what and who is right in front of me, and the words and emotions being shared.

Listening past the hurt allows me to consider what else may be going on in someone's life. I consider the possibility that the words that feel and sound so negatively directed toward me may have absolutely nothing to do with me at all. It allows me to have more compassion and grace toward others."

Journaling is a cathartic and spiritual practice for Amy. You can set the conditions for a successful journaling practice by establishing your own personal framework.

Your Journaling Invitation

Whether you are journaling to reap the benefits, manage stress, or as a creative outlet, allow yourself the freedom to express yourself in a safe and supportive environment. By providing a platform for self-expression, reflection, and growth, journaling offers many benefits and serves as a highly effective and accessible wellness modality. Consider incorporating regular journaling into your life for positive change and long-lasting wellness benefits.

Journaling Reflection Questions:

1. Have you ever used journaling as a wellness tool? If so, what has your experience been?

2. Were the prompts or techniques in this chapter helpful in organizing your thoughts?

TOM'S STORYBOARD
The Water's Edge

Chaos	Drill Sergeant Demands
Anchor	The Water's Edge
Calm	Personal Mantra of "Giver"

The alarm blared at 0400, or four o'clock in the morning, like it did every day on the trail, signaling the start of another long shift. As a drill sergeant, my life revolved around discipline, intensity, and long hours. By 0500, I was already at work before the trainees even stirred. By 1500, I'd already clocked eleven hours, but the day was far from over. Seven more hours of issuing orders, correcting forms, and driving home the details of military precision awaited me.

When I finally got home, it meant five hours of sleep and barely any family time. The job takes a toll, and I quickly learned the importance of releasing the pressure—blowing off steam. I did not want to carry the intensity home to my family.

On one of many scorching summer days at Fort Sill, Oklahoma, we had just returned from a field training exercise. Everyone was sweat drenched, sticky, and ready for some kind of relief. My office offered no reprieve from the heat—no air conditioning. But I had one small comfort waiting for me: a KitKat bar. I'd been saving the candy and was ready to eat it. When I opened the wrapper, the sight of the melted candy bar greeted me in gooey defiance. The other drill sergeants started laughing as I tried to salvage a messy bite.

With chocolate and wafer bits clinging to my fingers, I paused, smiled, and said, "Let's have some fun with this."

Marching out to the barracks, I shouted, "What squad is in charge of the latrines?"

A few soldiers came running, nervous and unsure.

"Everyone, get over here!" I barked. "These latrines are disgusting!"

Now, in truth, the latrines were spotless. The recruits had scrubbed them so thoroughly that they practically sparkled. If this had been a television commercial, you'd see those little animated twinkles of cleanliness. But that wasn't the point. With a dozen young soldiers crowded around the bathroom stalls, I had their full attention.

Dramatically, I knelt by a toilet bowl, dragged two clean fingers along the rim, but I held up my two chocolate-coated fingers.

"What is this?" I demanded. "It looks like shit!"

The soldiers froze, their faces went pale—it was utter disbelief. Then I took it a step further. I sniffed my chocolate-coated fingers.

"Smells like shit," I said, holding back my own laughter.

And then, with exaggerated theatrics, I stuck my fingers in my mouth.

"Tastes like shit!" I announced.

Savoring the moment, I rubbed the chocolate "evidence" all over my teeth for good measure. You could've heard a pin drop in that barracks. The soldiers were horrified, staring at me as if I'd lost my mind. My fellow drill sergeants could barely keep from laughing, and I knew the recruits would be talking about this for days.

Later, I overheard whispers in the hall: "Is that the drill sergeant who ate shit?"

I never confirmed or denied the rumor. Some mysteries are best left unsolved.

That night, I drove home with the lingering sweetness on my tongue and in my soul. Sometimes, humor is the best medicine. A good laugh helps me blow off steam and not take everything too seriously. I now live in Belize and the heat melts everything. My KitKat bars live in the freezer—an easy solution to a sticky problem.

# # # #

I got to know Tom virtually, and he invited me to his boutique hotel in Belize where I led two weeklong wellness retreats. He expressed curiosity about my practices and teachings. Overtime, he learned to be a wellness weaver.

The water's edge always comforts Tom. Whether he's at an inland lake, a Great Lake, an ocean, or a river, Tom experiences a calming shift from life's stressors to the present moment. He is drawn to the water when things feel frustrating, overwhelming, or sideways. If he needs to reset, the water gives his perspective back. An instant feeling of grounding covers him while he stands on the terraform as the water washes over his feet. You see, Tom lives in a tropical paradise exactly eighty feet from the sea, but he experienced avalanches in his daily life after he and his family made the bold decision to leave the United States and become owners of a boutique hotel on the Placencia Peninsula of Belize. The transition was difficult. The move was a total disruption to their life.

He reflects, "We planned, changed environments, and moved away from all of our family and friends."

The hotel renovation and startup challenges were magnified by the COVID-19 pandemic lockdown and supply chain backlogs. Tom describes his daily avalanche as "that mid-day moment when all the things my wife Lori and I knew were going wrong hit a crescendo." Independently, each problem was not a big deal but collectively felt like a snowslide. Not having the same, ready access to resources as when living in the states proved incredibly frustrating.

In the crush of an avalanche, Tom has learned to walk down to the beach until he connects with the water. With warm waves barely covering his feet, and then decisively receding, his worries lighten and fade. The water tirelessly ebbs and flows. The tide forever rubbing back and forth across the sand is frustratingly consistent and never ending. Tom repeatedly returns to the water. If it is over one hundred degrees, if someone dies or is born, or if five doors need redoing, the tide does not care, it just continues its cadence. Tom counts on it being the same. He knows the water can take his life or save his life; it has no emotion . . . just energy. Tom's peace comes from the understanding that what was bothering him at that exact moment is not a big deal. The water does not care and acts like an emotional eraser as it moves back and forth over Tom's feet.

He shares, "My entire perspective shifts as I stand still and watch the simple, constant, back and forth action."

As a former U.S. Army Drill Instructor, Tom appreciates and prefers consistency. As a Sergeant, everything needed to be the same, dress-right-dress. Consistency is now woven into his life. He has three pairs of shorts, and he rotates them. If they wear out, he buys three more of the same shorts. He enjoys the same restaurant food and drink. This life is not boring for him; it is comforting. Tom does not mind trying new things but recedes like the waves to what is familiar and comfortable.

Consistently, Tom sits for up to an hour if needed, gazing at the sea water in silence as he sips his fresh orange juice from the local juice delivery guy, and awaits the possibility of a midday avalanche. When it hits, he moves to the water's edge and stands on white, iridescent sand pocked with fossils. The shallow water and constant tide protect the few pieces of 100-year-old coral visible from the shoreline. There is a predictable quiet—a mixture of subtle cleansing waves washing over the sand, black birds changing tree branches, and a parrot that sporadically yells, "Mama!" that engulfs Tom.

The grounding sensation melts away Tom's wintery Wisconsin backstory. Having moved somewhere else for paradise, the avalanches still follow. When the sense of unease casts a shadow, Tom, craving consistency and predictability, moves to the water's edge alone. If a long time passes, Lori comes down to check on him or to provide an update on the day's avalanche activity. She respects and protects Tom's time of reflection. She knows this stillness benefits their collective life.

Proximity to the water refreshes and maintains Tom's perspective. He is grateful for life on the peninsula. Alone on the water's edge, Tom feels the somatic shift, and the calmness refills his zest and zeal for running his business, caring for his family, and enjoying the salt life!

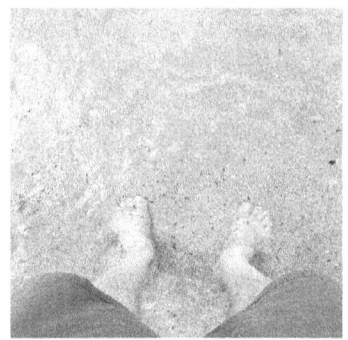

Poem
Water
Consistent, peaceful
Moving, cleansing, enduring
Subtle shift of perspective
Giver

Mantra
"Giver"

Tom's personal mantra is the word giver. By quietly revisiting his mantra whenever he needs a moment of calm, Tom can cultivate a sense of grounding.

CHAPTER 7
Prayer Power

Prayer is a powerful tool for connecting with something greater, grounding us in peace and purpose. Engaging in prayer is a powerful and accessible holistic practice to enhance mental, spiritual, and emotional well-being. Prayer is the act of speaking with God or a deity and often associated with religious traditions, structured rituals, and spirituality. The act of praying can take many forms; it can be silent, spoken, informal, formal, or repetitive. Prayers are real. They consist of thoughts and words, measurable brain activity. Thoughts and words comprising prayer are real, important, and shared by an individual or group to have a meaningful dialogue with the divine.

However, prayer extends beyond this traditional context and encompasses additional modalities, such as the following practices:

1. Moments of introspection, mindfulness, and solace
2. Expressions of gratitude and thanksgiving
3. Praise to God, gods, or an object
4. Solemn requests
5. Meditation
6. Solitude
7. Fasting

Reasons for Praying

People engage in prayer for a multitude of reasons. Some people seek guidance or comfort while others use prayer as a form of personal reflection. For me, personal prayer has evolved into a constant conversation with God throughout my day. I start my day by reading a passage in a devotional book filled with inspirational stories and scriptures, journaling three things I am grateful for to God, and listening to worship songs praising Jesus in my car. I continue by asking God to guide my steps and the Holy Spirit to filter the words that come out and into my body. I specifically pray over my dinner meal and before I fall asleep.

During the act of prayer, an individual may cultivate a deep sense of purpose and connection, express gratitude, or find peace. Prayer serves as a purposeful opportunity to privately examine one's thoughts and mental processes.

Amid life's chaos, prayer offers Marcy, a Jewish Synagogue President and friend, a sacred pause to gain perspective and emotional stability.

She explains, "Prayer is personal and always there for me in my time of need. I call on my strong Jewish faith like I would a dear and trusted friend. It guides my way through the hurt and chaos."

The act of prayer comforts Marcy during emotionally stressful events in her life.

Marcy shares, "Prayer is there for me when I struggle with the current and senseless wars in Israel and Ukraine and all the sadness and injustices in our world. My faith is always there for me, a constant companion like my breath."

Marcy makes prayer part of her personal wellness routine. She prays each night before dinner to show appreciation for her blessings. On the Sabbath, known as Shabbat, she prays and practices traditional rituals from sundown on Friday until sundown on Saturday. Marcy also prays episodically as a silent reflection anytime and anyplace she feels moved to do so.

Prayer connects my dear friend Dr. Amy Kay Powell, a Christian small group leader, with God. I refer to her as a prayer warrior. The practice of praying offers Amy the opportunity to pause and experience peace. A peace she describes as "illogical but undeniable." Amy regularly prays for others who are experiencing unexpected loss, sadness, or chaotic situations. Prayers provide Amy and those she prays for a consistent source of comfort and a wellspring of resilience.

After the unexpected death of Amy's husband Jon at age 47, she cultivated a practice of praying regularly and found her own church family.

Amy doesn't recall crying out to God after Jon's death, but she shares, "I do know, without any question or doubt, that God used individuals, their actions and prayers to comfort me, support me, and ultimately lead me to Athens Church where my faith and relationship with Him was nurtured and has grown exponentially."

She heartfeltly states, "Having others pray for me has been one the most powerful things I have experienced. I have seen and felt how God has answered those prayers in my life and in the lives of people close to me. Often, this has manifested incredible peace in the midst of intense grief, loss, or confusion."

Amy's favorite bible scripture is John 14:27 (WEB), "Peace I leave with you. My peace I give to you; not as the world gives, I give to you. Don't let your heart be troubled, neither let it be fearful."

She has embraced this peaceful verse since Jon's death after coming upon it multiple times from vastly different sources. Amy knew it was God's message for her, and she felt it was reassurance of His presence in her life.

Being on the receiving end of both comfort and peace, Amy shares, "I've come to know, believe, and trust in that God truly can use all things together for good. If I don't understand or agree with the way something is playing out in my life, I just stay in prayerful contact with God, following His lead and plan."

Amy prays for others as part of her daily living. Personal prayers and praying for others allow Amy to adapt better to adversity, to maintain equilibrium, and serve as her cornerstone for achieving inner peace.

Benefits of Prayer

Prayer is also a tool of connection bridging our human condition to our divine creator and one another. This holistic tool has many benefits. Some benefits are tangible and measurable while others are nonphysical and abstract.

Scientific studies suggest that regular prayer positively correlates with a wide array of health and well-being benefits. Let us examine some benefits positively affecting our well-being.

A National Institutes of Health study of Blue Zones, regions of the world where people regularly live for over one hundred years, identified nine commonalities of successful centenarians.

The study established, "About twenty percent of how long the average person lives is dictated by our genes, whereas the other eighty percent is dictated by our lifestyle."

The common link presented is being actively connected to a faith-based community.

Specifically, "All but five of the two hundred sixty-three centenarians interviewed belonged to some faith-based community." It was noted that religious denomination did not seem to matter. Research depicted, "Attending faith-based services four times per month will add four to fourteen years of life expectancy" (Buettner, et al. 2016).

Harvard Professors Tyler VanderWeele and Ying Chen led a large population study positively connecting "the association of religious involvement in adolescence (including religious service attendance and prayer or meditation) with a wide array of psychological well-being, mental health, health behavior, physical health, and character strength outcomes in young adulthood."

The researchers concluded, "Although decisions about religion are not shaped principally by health, encouraging service attendance and private practices in adolescents who already hold religious beliefs may be meaningful avenues of development and support, possibly leading to better health and well-being."

In the study, "Nearly sixty percent of the participants attended religious services at least weekly, and thirty-six percent reported prayer or meditation at least once per day."

The study noted, "All models were controlled for sociodemographic characteristics, maternal health, and prior values of the outcome variable whenever data were available" (Chen, et al. 2018).

Not all benefits are easily measured or evidenced-based; some are experiential.

Lieutenant Colonel Jimmy Bellamy, a US Army Chaplain and combat veteran shares, "Prayer helps some people avoid temptation, face adversity, overcome trials, and prosper. Most importantly, prayer helps people find meaning and gives them hope."

Military chaplains have the mission to offer religious support, service, and counseling to service members of many faiths.

Since they operate in this pluralistic environment, Chaplain Bellamy emphasizes, "The main thing is to respect each other's faith and boundaries."

By being transparent with God and other people, Chaplain Bellamy shows respect.

He shares this helpful prayer tip, "When you are praying, be transparent with God—you are talking to a deity. Someone you believe has a higher power. Someone you believe can get you through the difficult time."

Prayer is not a negotiation process. It is not about convincing God to change or converting others—it is about changing us at our core. While deployed, Chaplain Bellamy ensured the opportunity for four Muslim soldiers to use a local mosque for prayer. In return, the soldiers invited him to come in, and they all prayed together. Respect was both given and received.

Before Chaplain Bellamy leads community prayer, he says aloud, "I invite everyone to pray in their faith tradition as I pray in mine." He explains, "This allows people to believe in their supreme being."

For Chaplain Bellamy it is God and Jesus, for others it may be Budda, Allah, or other gods.

Types of Prayer

If you are new to prayer or struggle in your attempts to make your personal prayer meaningful, you have options ranging from formal prayers and songs to personal words and thoughts. At wellness retreats, I like to remind myself and others, we are spiritual beings having a physical experience together. To support and respect everyone in attendance, we offer time for reflection, the opportunity to pray aloud, and share a blessing or moment of silence over our food.

Prayers vary across religions and personal beliefs, but a few common types include:

- **Adoration:** Praising and glorifying a deity or object
- **Confession:** Acknowledging and seeking forgiveness and cleansing for wrongdoing
- **Lamentation:** Passionately expressing grief or sorrow.
- **Intercession:** Praying on others' behalf
- **Liturgy:** Formal prayers used in religious ceremonies and traditions
- **Meditation:** Reflection for spiritual growth
- **Petition:** Praying for specific needs or desires for self or others
- **Supplication:** Requests for divine guidance, mercy, grace or intervention
- **Thanksgiving:** Expressing gratitude for blessings

Each type of prayer serves different spiritual purposes and can be adapted to individual preferences. Research involving breast cancer survivors from different ethnic groups examined how the use of prayer is related to mood and quality of life. The study showed benefits for spiritual well-being among those who prayed.

Specifically, the data revealed, "Women who prayed were able to find more positive contributions from their cancer experience than women who did not pray." Petition, comfort, and praise prayers were the types of prayer used in this study (Levine, et al. 2009).

How to Pray

Now that we have defined prayer, shared the benefits, and explained different types, it is time to put prayer into action by sharing some examples of how to pray. In the Christian faith, the invitation to pray is repeatedly recorded in biblical scripture, yet followers of Christ struggled.

In Matthew 6:9-13, Jesus instructs his apostles how to pray by sharing The Lord's Prayer, also known as the Our Father Prayer. Application can feel awkward, but with practice you may feel more confident. Cultivating a personal prayer practice can enhance your wellness. Let's dive into some specifics examples and tips to help you get started.

The following examples and tips will guide you in cultivating a personal prayer practice.

Oaks Church Brooklyn's *The Good Way* offers the mnemonic device 'PRAY' as a helpful way to start a personal prayer practice. PRAY stands for the following actions: Pause, Rejoice, Ask, and Yield.[4]

- **P**ause: sit (optional: stand, kneel, or lie down) quietly and seek stillness.
- **R**ejoice: read something inspirational.
- **A**sk: tell God what is on your heart or on your mind.
- **Y**ield: read a few sacred verses.
- *Optional*: open and close your prayer with an appropriate salutation.

The PRAY tool may help you or others in developing a personal prayer practice and is adaptive for many of the world's religions.

Another prayer method is to use Breath Prayers where you use your inhale and exhale to express a short, repetitive prayer. During wellness retreats and for continued lifestyle well-being, I encourage the use of breath prayers as part of their client's yoga practice, stand-alone breathing practice, personal prayer, and reflection.

Inhale: (*insert personal prayer phrase here*)
Exhale: *(insert personal prayer phrase here)*
Repeat

Examples of prayers I have used for Breath Prayers are:

Inhale: Nourish
Exhale: Cleanse
Repeat for 3-5 breaths

Inhale: Every prayer today
Exhale: Is a seed for tomorrow
Repeat for 1-3 minutes
Inhale: I am
Exhale: Resilient (other exhale options: at peace, enough, grateful, on a journey, capable, strong, or word of your choice)
Repeat for 1-3 minutes

Additional Prayer Tips:

- ➢ Identify an appropriate time in your day to support consistent practice.
- ➢ Find a comfortable seated or kneeling position.
- ➢ Bring palms together over the heart center or another comfortable position.
- ➢ Begin with a greeting and know who you are talking with.
- ➢ Give praise to God and thanks for the blessings in your life.
- ➢ Pray specifically for yourself and others.
- ➢ Read a scripture, meaningful devotion, or poem.

Your Prayer Invitation

Whether through structured religious rituals or quiet personal reflections, integrating prayer into daily life can contribute to a more balanced and resilient sense of well-being. Prayer as a consistent practice provides a steady source of strength, enabling individuals to navigate stressors with greater ease and resilience. Prayer has shown to enhance one's ability to face life's uncertainties and daily living. Prayer is a powerful and accessible holistic wellness practice for people worldwide. Consider incorporating prayer into your life for positive change and long-lasting wellness benefits.

The Power of Prayer Reflection Questions:

1. How has prayer or meditation shaped your wellness practices?

2. Were you able to integrate the techniques suggested in this chapter into your daily routine? Why or why not?

COURTNEY'S STORYBOARD
Predawn Coffee

Chaos	Undercover Police Work
Anchor	Yellowstone
Calm	Personal Mantra of "Relaxation"

When I volunteered to be a decoy in a prostitution sting, it was about determination, not adventure. Prostitution and related crimes saturated my patrol sector. I saw an opportunity to take a new approach. People often think of prostitutes as big-city women, dolled up in flashy outfits with dramatic hair and makeup. That's an HBO movie, not Athens, Georgia. Here, it's jeans, a T-shirt, and a lollipop—a Blow Pop, to be exact. Nothing fancy, nothing glamorous.

I was confident with my team and mission. We were a resource intensive team, but everyone was experienced. The support crew consisted of a three-person team in a van, all with backgrounds in drug and vice operations. They observed, surveilled, and recorded. I was wearing a microphone, so they could hear everything. I had a little fun with that while I was walking alone. The takedown team included two uniformed officers in marked police cars, ready to swoop in at the first mention of our code phrase: "Fire in the hole."

Georgia law is clear—no entrapment. I could not suggest anything or corner anyone into solicitation. It had to be their idea. So, I hit the street, lollipop in hand, and started walking. I wasn't sure what to say at first. What kind of "street slang" sounds normal? I had practiced a few lines, but every encounter was unpredictable.

Sometimes, I'd just smile and say, "Hey baby, how you doing?" or "I really like your hair."

Simple compliments kept the conversation going. The experienced "Johns" would recognize the stall tactic and take off.

Others would engage by asking me questions like, "What are you doing out here?" or "Do you want to go somewhere?"

Some gave me compliments: "You look hot. Can I take you to dinner?"

I always played it coy.

"What do you mean? Where do you want to go? How would I pay for that?"

My team joked that men are suckers, pun intended. The lollipop became a prop! Just licking the candy was enough to draw attention.

"What flavor is that?" the John would ask, or even worse, "Would you do that to me?"

That's when they would get to the point.

"How much would it cost me?" they would ask.

I wasn't a high-class prostitute. My services were pretty much $25. Once they made an offer, I would casually drop the code phrase into the conversation and start walking away. The takedown team would roll in, arrest the guy, and move on to the next one. In one day, we'd catch four or five Johns. The only reason we would stop was the paperwork—it was overwhelming. The men we caught included teachers, husbands, businessmen, and even a church official—most were married.

The operation was effective but incredibly resource intensive. Eventually, the department scaled the operation back to once a year, moving it to a different shift and sector. But the game changed. Solicitation started moving online. On game days in Athens, the city became a hotspot for prostitution. The deals were digital. It's all online, grimy, and exposed. Looking back, I'm glad I could help take some creeps off the streets. Those men were gross.

# # # #

Courtney cofounded and served as the executive director of the Georgia Association of Women in Public Safety. She invited me to provide a wellness event for its board of directors to improve resilience. I quickly recognized this high-ranking law enforcement official also could benefit from weaving wellness into her daily routine.

In need of a vacation, Courtney became intrigued with the creation of the United States National Parks System. Development of the parks system began as a presidential program to create jobs and became a legacy piece of history, preservation, and solace for all beings. Yellowstone, in its geothermal glory, was the first national park. Naturally, it was Courtney's first pick for a hard-earned vacation from law enforcement duty.

For seven carefree days, Courtney and her wife called a massive log cabin home. Together as visitors, they witnessed geological wonders. Their eyes drank in travertine terraces and angry fumaroles releasing their hot steam. In the hydrothermal basins, thermophiles matted together in spectacular color. For these microscopic heat lovers, the hot springs are home.

Courtney could feel her pace slowing and breath deepening hoping the vacation would deliver on all its promises.

As sour geysers burped, there was no escaping the lingering sulfur smell. Eggs for breakfast, anyone?

Suddenly, a high-pitched bugle was heard! Among rustling trees, a cow elk vocalizes, "I'm aroused and ready!"

As a police chief, Courtney could relate to the hypervigilant elk. Courtney's nervous system defaulted to being aware of and prepared for any scenario. This seasoned vigilance saved her life once and prevented injury (or limited harm) throughout her career. With a big exhale, Courtney reminded herself she was on vacation, and the elk was not a threat.

As a reserved person, Courtney found comfort being alone, and protection in small groups, especially her law enforcement pack. She regularly stepped out of her comfort zone without hesitation and similarly perfected disappearing back to her own solace or the pack's comfort with ghost-like precision. In the park, everyone was highly social, active, and vying for the best view or position. She observed the crowd moving about in their own packs. In the cool evening at their echoey lodge, visitors all came together to share meals, play boardgames, and craft plans for tomorrow. The cabin provided basic provisions . . . it was simple and enough.

In the serene darkness of the early morning, Courtney found a calm space as she nestled closer to her steaming sweetened coffee. The relit morning fire gave off a charred, earthy smell while she scanned the local newspaper. Courtney's predawn darkness in the park was uninterrupted and comfortable. Ah, this craved solace refreshed her entire being.

There is a lull before sunrise; a pause for her to think, be, and know. Being alone in the morning provided Courtney with a predictable pattern of complete relaxation, no external worries.

With a closed-lipped smile, she silently proclaims with coffee cup in hand, "Today will be good!"

Courtney continues the grounding practice of predawn coffee. In the busyness of life and the shadows of danger, she can turn her thoughts inward to rest and refresh. Yellowstone memories are Courtney's solemn touchstone for dialing down. It is also her benchmark for all other national parks. She can still hear the echoes of the elk bugling.

Poem
Yellowstone
dynamic, geological
erupting, drinking, watching
crisp and vibrant wonders
relaxation

Mantra
"Relaxation"

Courtney's personal mantra is the word relaxation. By quietly revisiting her mantra whenever she needs a moment of calm, Courtney can cultivate a sense of grounding.

CHAPTER 8
Weaving it All Together for Balance

The journey to balance starts with the power to create your own path to peace. As we come to the end of our journey together, it is time to take what you have learned and create your own personal wellness routine tailored to your unique needs and circumstances. Throughout this book, you have read stories of our everyday heroes cultivating their personal mantras and explored evidence-based holistic wellness approaches to move from chaos to calm. Now, the power is in your hands.

This chapter invites you to reflect on a grounding anchor that cultivates peace, develop a personal mantra to guide you back to calm, and weave together your own wellness practices to live the dialed-down life.

Your Grounding Anchor and Personal Mantra

Let's cultivate an inner calmness you can access regularly. Begin by finding a quiet space to reflect on a grounding anchor— a real place that brings you peace, connection, and stability. It could be a memory, a favorite place in nature, or even a simple object. Take a moment to journal or silently describe your anchor using your five senses and noticing how you feel.

- What do you see? Notice color, contrast, and more.
- What do you touch? Notice what textures, shapes, or colors stand out?
- What do you hear? Can you pick up sounds close and far?
- What do you smell? Is there a pungent or lingering scent?
- How does it make you feel? Sit and notice until a feeling arises.

Let the stillness settle in as you focus on your anchor. When you are ready, use your anchor to craft a five-line Cinquain poem to formulate a personal mantra, a repeated word, aligned with your breath, used silently or aloud to focus the mind and foster calmness. Each line builds upon your connection to the anchor:

Line 1: Write a noun naming your anchor.

Line 2: Write two adjectives describing your anchor.

Line 3: Write three verbs (often ending in 'ing') that bring you to your anchor.

Line 4: Write a four-word phrase that reflects your feelings or additional information about the anchor.

Line 5: Write one synonym (closely associated word) for your anchor that sums up your experience

The final word of your poem becomes your personal mantra. Use your mantra as a simple, meaningful guide to recenter and restore balance daily or on demand. As you repeat your mantra, silently or softly aloud, begin to align the word with your breath. Explore inhaling deeply and exhaling fully as you say your mantra, or vice versa. Use your breath aligned mantra to focus the mind and foster calmness.

Personal Mantra: (Insert your word from Line 5)

Using a Personal Mantra to Cultivate Inner Calmness

A personal mantra can be a powerful tool to reset your mind, refocus your energy, and restore balance. The word or short phrase serves to ground and calm—a simple yet meaningful guide for navigating life's chaos. The mantra, aligned with your breath, can help you foster calmness and clarity.

Below are five steps to help you incorporate your personal mantra into your daily life:

1. **Choose Your Mantra with Intention.** Select a word or short phrase that deeply resonates with you. For this book's framework, your mantra is the final word of your poem. It should embody your desired sense of grounding, balance, or focus. Examples include "peace," "strength," or "calm."

2. **Find a Quiet Moment.** Take a few moments in a space where you feel comfortable and uninterrupted. You can sit or stand, close your eyes if it feels natural, and begin to turn your focus inward. If you're in a busy or noisy environment, take a few slow, deep breaths to center yourself before continuing.

3. **Align Your Mantra with Your Breath.** Silently or softly, repeat your mantra in rhythm with your breath. On an inhale, think or say your mantra to yourself. On the exhale, imagine releasing tension or anything that no longer serves you. Alternatively, inhale positivity and exhale the mantra itself. Explore which pattern feels the most grounding for you. Let the repetition create a calming cadence in your mind.

4. **Feel Its Presence.** As you repeat your mantra, focus on the sensations it evokes. Let its meaning settle into your thoughts and body. For example, if your mantra is "peace," imagine a wave of peaceful energy spreading through you with every breath. Allow this connection to deepen with each repetition. Perhaps you begin your mantra practice with three to five iterations and work your way up to three to five minutes.

5. **Revisit Your Mantra Throughout the Day.** Your mantra is not limited to moments of meditation. Return to it anytime you need to recenter, whether during a stressful situation, while transitioning between tasks, or before bed.

Even a few seconds of silently repeating your mantra can bring you back to a place of calm and focus.

A Daily Practice for Balance

Using your mantra regularly, whether for a few moments or as part of a longer practice, can help ground you in the present and bring clarity to your day. This gentle technique empowers you to refocus, reduce stress, and cultivate a sense of calm whenever life feels overwhelming.

By incorporating these steps, you can make your mantra a practical and meaningful part of your daily routine. Let it be a guide to help you align with balance and calm whenever needed. For additional worksheets to craft your grounding anchor and personal mantra, see Appendix C - Personal Mantra Framework.

My Storyboard: Breakwater Lighthouse

Grounding anchors change according to the season of life you are in. Early in my military career, I deployed and moved around frequently. At times, I felt a little untethered, like a small boat on the moody waves of Lake Michigan. I had my unit and battle buddy, but my family and childhood friends—those who really know me—were in my hometown of Manitowoc, Wisconsin.

Thoughts of watching the rotating Fresnel lens of the Breakwater Lighthouse cast light along the pier and shoreline of my hometown comforted me. Even now, my breath can easily fall in synchronization with the towering light's cadence.

The poem that follows describes my grounding anchor—the lighthouse. The last line of the poem reveals my personal mantra—support. By meditating on my word "support," I could cultivate the comforting feeling of being supported, rooted back to my hometown, and steadfast like the lighthouse. No matter where my journey took me, I knew my boat could always return to a safe harbor—home.

Poem
*Lighthouse
Strong, bright
Towering, warning, guiding
Steadfast in all seasons
Support*

Mantra
"Support"

My personal mantra in this season of life was the word support. By quietly revisiting my mantra whenever I needed a moment of calm, I could cultivate a sense of grounding.

Designing Your Wellness Routine

With your mantra in mind, consider how you can integrate the wellness practices we have explored into your daily life and weekly routine. Here are the key takeaways from each chapter to inspire your routine:

Yoga and Breath Practices: Harmony for Body, Mind, and Spirit. Yoga does not require perfection. It can be as simple as a few mindful breaths each day, an at home practice, or a traditional yoga class in a studio. Yoga offers your mind and body a chance to achieve harmony, providing long-lasting benefits like reduced stress, increased flexibility, and inner calm. Incorporate yoga as it fits your life. Start small and let it flow and grow!

Nature's Goodness: Reconnect with the Outdoors. Mother nature offers countless benefits from cleaner air and reduced stress to improved clarity and immunity. Whether you choose to forest bathe, garden, walk, or birdwatch, making time for nature fosters balance and wellness. Choose an outdoor activity that interests you. Remember, choice is empowering! Mother nature is waiting for you.

Whole Foods, Plant-based Eating: Food to Fuel and Feel Good! A plant-based diet focused on whole foods and proper hydration enhances wellness by nourishing the body and mind. While there is no perfect diet, small shifts—like adding more vegetables, whole grains, and hydration—can make a significant difference. Use the recipe as a kickstart and the tips in this book to begin crafting meals that both nurture and energize you and those you care for and love.

Journaling: A Safe Space for Growth. Journaling allows you to manage stress, reflect, and express yourself creatively. By providing a private space for your thoughts, journaling fosters self-awareness and growth. Begin with a few minutes a day or once a week to explore your emotions, dreams, or gratitude. Let each page hold your mindful words.

Prayer: A Source of Resilience and Strength. Whether through structured rituals or personal reflections, prayer offers a profound sense of balance and calm. Prayer provides a steady source of strength and resilience, helping you navigate life's challenges. Find a comfortable time or a few moments each day to pray or meditate. Choose a time that feels comfortable for you. This practice grounds you in the present and connects you to your deeper purpose.

Creating Your Wellness Routine

Use the *Flow into Balance* chart on page 120 to plan your week, incorporating elements from each practice that resonate most with you. As the chart suggests, think of inviting movement, harmony, energy, and a grounded calmness into your life. The chart intentionally provides mantra integration.

Write in your personal mantra, or mantra for the week or this season of life, to reflect on while practicing a wellness modality. You have room to make customizable entries. Each week, jot down specific activities, actions, and reflections to explore and practice. Keep it easy and flexible; this is a wellness practice and not a plan to be perfectly executed. However, feel free to add your own flavor to the chart such as color-coding sections to enhance usability (Appendix D – Color Coding).

Use what nurtures you. The chart places the days of the week at the top and the wellness practices vertically, with a space for your mantra at the bottom. As you flow into balance with your personal wellness routine, notice your internal shift from chaos to calm. Small, intentional steps create a ripple of calm and connection through your week.

How I Weave It All Together!

Here is a glimpse of my daily wellness activities that I currently weave into my week. Use this as an example and not *the* example. To work effectively for you, it needs to fit your life circumstances and season of life. These are the activities that I put on my *Flow into Balance* chart.

My activities include a few wellness practices for each category:

Yoga and Breathwork: Do a minimum of ten minutes of morning yoga upon waking up; belly breathing in my car while running errands; restorative forward fold while walking my dogs; and legs up the wall pose for five minutes before bed. Additionally, I teach three yoga classes a week.

Nature Immersion: I regularly walk my dogs in the neighborhood; occasionally drink my coffee outside with my bare feet on the grass; and routinely take time to notice the sunrise and watch the sunset.

Plant-based Eating: I prepare meals for the week on Sunday; eat a hearty bowl of oatmeal or vegan yogurt daily with all the fixings; and share one meatless meal with a friend. Additionally, I maintain a ninety-plus percent plant-based intake.

Journaling: I write three things I am grateful for daily and make one reflective entry of the joys of my week.

Prayer: I lift up all the prayers from my small group, pray over our family's evening meal, and reflect on Psalm 28:7 (WEB), "The Lord is my strength and my shield. My heart has trusted in him, and I am helped. Therefore my heart greatly rejoices." With my song I will thank him. A psalm is a sacred song, and I had this one tattooed on my forearm when going through a difficult time in my life.

Connection Activity: I host Taco Tuesday for friends; attend bible study small group; and actively listen in a meaningful conversation.

Current Personal Mantra: Ease.

Now it is your turn to make a list of activities and put them on your weekly wellness map below with your personal mantra. You do not have to do one for each section every day. Make it work for you and this season of life. Be a wellness weaver! Explore weaving wellness practices into your daily routine to both cultivate calmness and reclaim balance.

Craft Your Wellness Routine!

Flow into Balance: Your Weekly Wellness Map							
Practice	Sunday	Monday	Tuesday	Wednesday	Thursday	Friday	Saturday
Yoga and Breathwork							
Nature Immersion							
Plant-based Eating							
Journaling							
Prayer (or Meditation)							
Connection Activity							
Mantra:							

Moving Forward

Take this moment to celebrate how far you have come. By integrating your personal mantra as you weave together these wellness practices into your life, you are creating a roadmap to a more grounded, balanced, and calm life. Remember, this is your practice. It can evolve with time and grow as you do. As you journey forward, return to your mantra whenever you need to re-center yourself. Let it remind you of the peace and strength you carry within, always available to guide you back to calm.

Your path to wellness begins now. You've got this!

Weaving It All Together Reflection Questions

1. Which combination of practices discussed in the book feels most accessible to you?

2. How might integrating multiple wellness practices impact your daily life?

DAVE'S STORYBOARD
The Fire Pit

Chaos	Classified Military Operation
Anchor	Fire Pit
Calm	Personal Mantra of "Family"

In 2004, my three-man team became the first Department of Defense element of its kind to deploy to Paktika Province, Afghanistan, in support of Joint Special Operations Command elements. We were creating the playbook as we went, the enemy was unpredictable. Some days, we would sit on a rug in a mud hut near the Afghanistan-Pakistan border, eating rice with our hands from a communal pan. Often, we shared these meals with village elders or local warlords, surrounded by their personal militias. Other nights, I would find myself fully kitted out: helmet, body armor, and multiple firearms. At 0400, four o'clock in the morning, I would be on the edge of a perimeter, postured and ready, waiting for the team's breacher to blow the doors of a walled compound so we could reach a high-value target.

Across multiple deployments, the basic mission never changed, but the operational profile always did. On one deployment, we rolled out as a two-man team in a locally purchased commercial vehicle, dressed in indigenous clothing to blend in with the local population. The goal was to avoid drawing any unwanted attention or suspicion. I carried an M4 carbine concealed in the vehicle and a Sig Sauer 9mm hidden under my garments. My unarmed interpreter, or "terp," made up the other half of our team. Technically, terps weren't allowed to carry weapons. Resources were limited, and backup wasn't always readily available. If things went sideways, the terp and I would hunker down at a pre-identified hardstand—a defensible position or structure—until help arrived. On every deployment, the stakes were high, and constant vigilance was the norm. There was little time to reflect or process. Those moments would come later.

# # # #

After five deployments to Afghanistan, Dave needed to decompress. However, the confidential nature of his work prevented him from talking about his military service in detail. I helped him reflect on his experiences to uncover his grounding anchor.

The fresh wood fire pit, glowing reddish orange, was the cultural conduit to all his previous combat deployments. Just thinking of the four-foot-wide ring painted dirt beige on a remote compound triggered a flashback to the best team and group of terps Dave calls family.

"Drop your gear and gather round!" was his easygoing command.

The highly skilled and determined military team exchanged tactical kits of weapons and body armor for cigars, refreshments, and bottles of water. They craved sleep and were shower deprived for days. Pushing past their own discomfort, the team gathered around the fire pit to stave off post-mission isolation.

With crackling wood for music, green tea—some infused with a hint of contraband bourbon, spoken words were barely shared. Each seasoned warrior sensed the quiet relief of everyone returning to base and the comfort of everyone being in the same safe place. Dave knew the importance of conducting buddy checks. Carving out time to decompress together trumped nature's call for sleep. With the warmth of the fire and tea, everyone shared stories. The gathering cultivated a welcoming calmness for everyone.

Dave whispers, "This is good for my guys."

Suddenly, a great debate broke out over the adornments on the fire pit's rim that safely held their dusty boots and tainted tea.

At full squint, a sleepy-eyed warrior whispered, "I see eyeballs and maybe penises" while another declared "Oh no, those are arrows and nipples." More rational minds suggested it surely represents "a heart leaving the fire pit going out into the mountains, like a soldier on a mission." Hmmm, perhaps it's not a peaceful prayer. The team settled on labeling the designs as "strange phallic symbols." Humor tore off the heavy veil of the danger they faced. Gathered around the fire pit, the feeling was lighter.

The team was safe after another avowed and hush-hush mission. The team provided villagers, elders, and children with one more night of sweat-earned safety and peace. The team's lingering and cajoling together kept their minds from worrying about wives, moms, babies, and life back in another world. The gathering reinforced that each man was essential, connected, and part of this family. Sleep came easier for each warrior. Thereafter, everyone migrated to the consoling fire pit. The gathering became the unit's standing post-mission practice, a ritual. Decompression achieved!

At his ranch-style home in Georgia where his home seamlessly blends with the natural surroundings, Dave built a rustic fire pit in his fenced-in backyard. The harmonious fusion of woodland elements and modern comforts creates a serene oasis for his entire family. Now, with a bourbon in hand, decompression is only a wood stack away.

Poem
Fire
hot, lively
resetting, consoling, bonding
conduit to cultural cohesion
family

Mantra
"Family"

Dave's personal mantra is the word family. By quietly revisiting his mantra whenever he needs a moment of calm, Dave can cultivate a sense of grounding.

CHAPTER 9
Living Your Best Dialed-Down Life

Living your best life starts with choosing calm over chaos, one intentional moment at a time. As you step into your new wellness journey, remember that living the dialed-down life is not about perfection; it's about intention. Recognize the tools you now hold and use them to transform moments of chaos into opportunities for calm.

Each practice shared in these pages, whether a deep breath, a quiet walk in nature, or a silent prayer, is a steppingstone toward a life rooted in balance and ever-growing resilience. You have the power to create this calm, no matter what storms come your way. Embrace the process, celebrate your small victories, and trust that every intentional choice leads you closer to a life of peace and connection. Your journey is uniquely yours. The calm you seek is already within you, ready to guide you to balance.

As I reflect on my own journey, I am reminded of how often I tend to overpack my suitcase, both literally and figuratively. During my cancer journey, well-meaning people offered advice, shared opinions about what I should or should not do and occasionally gifted me pearls of wisdom from their own experiences. I listened, grateful for their concern, but I quickly realized I could not carry everything. Instead, I picked up and used what best fit for my life situation and let go of the rest.

Over time, I pieced together my own wellness prescription, a recipe for life and survivorship. Just like an airline charge for heavy and excessive baggage, I didn't want my well-being to pay the price. I let go of the excess, kept what landed with me, and turned inward time and time again. Ease is my personal mantra, and I try to infuse it into my daily activities . . . and ease doesn't mean easy. By reflecting and repeating the word ease, I receive encouragement to keep trying, to add some space for perspective, and to exhale more deeply.

That recipe worked then and continues to work now, and I have dedicated myself to sharing it with others through role modeling lifestyle changes and the programs offered by Humble Warrior (Appendix F - Humble Warrior Wellness & Yoga Nonprofit).

My hope is that as you explore the practices in this book you will approach them like ingredients for your own wellness recipe. Some may want to ground themselves with an anchor; others will draft a personal mantra or put into practice a weekly wellness routine. Feel free to pick and choose and leave the rest.

Like any new journey, this process may feel exciting at first, but it can also bring challenges. Change is not always easy. Many of us are trained to do rather than to be, especially in careers that demand relentless action, such as the military, first responders, or healthcare. Resilience and well-being, however, often require a different rhythm. As you weave together your wellness routine, allow a rhythm to unfold that supports self-compassion, patience, and permission to care for yourself as you are.

Through Humble Warrior Wellness & Yoga, I have spent nearly a decade guiding individuals through evidence-based, trauma-informed frameworks. And now, you hold these tools in your hands!

Use this book not as a rigid guide but as a resource to support your unique journey. Show up for yourself exactly as you are and trust your intuition to take what you need and leave what does not serve you. This is not about fixing what is wrong with you; it is about nurturing what's right within you.

It is okay to feel uncertain or overwhelmed at times. Trust that clarity will come in its own time, often when you least expect it. By creating space for routine practice, you can find a steady rhythm, one where presence replaces pressure and calmness replaces chaos. The more you practice, the more this calmness grows, dose by dose. With each step, you move closer to an inner quiet where stillness meets ease.

As the Native American proverb reminds us: "Listen to the wind; it talks. Listen to the silence; it speaks. Listen to your heart; it knows."

Take your time, trust the process, and let your journey unfold as it is meant to.

Living Your Best Dialed-Down Life Reflection Questions:

1. What does a "dialed-down life" look like for you? Your family or friend group?

2. What small, sustainable changes can you make today to move closer to this vision?

APPENDIX A:
The Eight Limbs of Yoga Overview

The actual yoga postures, or poses, are just a small part of the larger practice that includes philosophy, ethics, breathwork, and meditation. The Eight Limbs of Yoga, as expounded in the Yoga Sutras of Patanjali Maharishi, provide a comprehensive framework for both the practice and philosophy of yoga (Satchidananda 2012).

Below is a concise overview of each limb and a simple example.

- Yamas (Ethical Standards of Abstinence). Yamas are moral principles guiding our conduct towards others and the world. One example, Ahimsa, or non-violence, advocates compassion towards all beings.

- Niyamas (Ethical Standards of Observance). Niyamas focus on personal observances and self-discipline. One example, Saucha, or cleanliness, encourages the purification of body and mind.

- Asanas (Physical Posture Practice). Asanas are the physical postures practiced in yoga to cultivate strength, flexibility, and balance in the body. Asana helps prepare the body for meditation.

- Pranayama (Breath Control). Pranayama involves breathing techniques or practices to control the flow of prana, or life force energy. One example, Ujjayi, or victorious breath, is a throat constriction-type of breathing sounding like ocean waves, used to calm the mind and energize the body.

- Pratyahara (Sensory Withdrawal). Pratyahara is the withdrawal of the senses from external stimuli. One example, turning our attention inward cultivates introspection and supports meditation.

- Dharana (Concentration). Dharana is the practice of having a single point of focus. One example, Tratak, or candle gazing, is to be fully absorbed in focusing on a single object, such as a candle.

- Dhyana (Meditation). Dhyana is a state of sustained awareness and effortless concentration. This limb taps into the mental activity of the mind such as your self-awareness, contemplation, and reflection. For example, focusing on a candle can evolve into feeling one with the flame.

- Samadhi (Superconscious State). Samadhi is the state of oneness, or union, where you achieve a sense of unity with all existence. You experience a reality without the constructed filter from all your life experiences or equanimity. One example, the state of bliss allows for a sense of joyful calmness or liberation.

These limbs form a progressive path guiding practitioners towards self-awareness, inner peace, and ultimately union.

APPENDIX B:
Types of Yoga

Yoga types are primarily named for the degree of physical intensity, cultural origin, or for the person creating the specific style of yoga practice. Collectively, the different types provide the opportunity to unite your body, mind, and spirit to enhance your overall wellbeing. Here are several types of yoga I've explored and their associated purposes:

Meditation is traditionally a seated or lying practice that involves focusing the mind to achieve a state of mental clarity, emotional calmness, and peace. It can be practiced in various forms, including object meditation where you observe a particular object such as a candle or a plant with a soft gaze; guided visualization where another person provides verbal cues such as tensing and relaxing a muscle; or as a themed meditation focusing on a thought, quality, or activity such as loving-kindness.

Yoga Nidra is a guided practice of systematic relaxation using body and breath awareness and visualization techniques to promote relaxation and enhance sleep. It is typically practiced lying down and aims to induce a state of deep relaxation. A pioneering study published in The Journal of Alternative and Complementary Medicine explored the efficacy of iRest, a trademarked form of Yoga Nidra by Dr. Richard Miller, as a complementary therapy for chronic combat-related post-traumatic stress disorder (PTSD). His research showed meaningful improvement in PTSD symptoms in a group of veterans (Miller, et al. 2012).

Restorative is a slow, gentle practice involving fewer poses, supported by props, and aimed at deep relaxation and stress reduction.

Chair is an effective and accessible practice for a wide range of people. Traditional yoga poses and stretches are modified for a sitting position. It aims at increased circulation, range of motion, strength, and cultivates a feeling of well-being.

Yin is a slow-paced, deep stretching practice where poses are held for longer durations, typically ranging from one to five minutes or more. These long holds target deeper connective tissues of the body to include ligaments, fascia, and scar tissue and are meant to stimulate the channels of the subtle body, known as meridians. The aim is to increase flexibility and promote relaxation.

Gentle is a mild practice of yoga typically suitable for all levels, beginners to senior practitioners. It focuses on slow, gentle movements, stretching, and breathing techniques to improve flexibility, balance, and to cultivate relaxation without putting undue stress on the body.

Hatha is an ancient traditional practice focusing on physical postures and breathing techniques to balance the body and mind.

Kundalini is a practice involving chanting, breathing exercises, and repetitive poses directed toward the release of latent energy believed to lie coiled at the base of the spine.

Iyengar, a trademarked practice based on the teaching of B.K.S. Iyengar, emphasizes the precise alignment of poses and commonly uses props to support the body. The aim is to promote and enhance both flexibility and stability.

Bikram is a trademarked practice consisting of 26 patented postures and two breathing exercises practiced in a heated room. This is a form of hot yoga where yoga is practiced in a heated room, typically between 90 to 105 degrees Fahrenheit (32 to 40 degrees Celsius), with high humidity. The aim is to enhance flexibility and detoxification.

Ashtanga is a rigorous practice that follows a specific or set sequence of poses. It emphasizes breath and movement coordination. The aim is to increase both strength and flexibility.

Vinyasa is a fast-paced dynamic practice where poses smoothly flow from one to the next, synchronized with the breath. The aim is to improve energy, strength, and flexibility.

Trauma-Sensitive Yoga is an adapted style of teaching complimenting existing practices with an emphasis on creating a safe and supportive environment for individuals who have experienced trauma. Teaching cues emphasize mindful movement, body awareness, and empowerment without triggering or re-traumatizing participants. The yoga teacher typically offers choices, avoids physical adjustments, and fosters a sense of agency and self-regulation.

APPENDIX C:
Personal Mantra Framework

The document provides a framework for creating a personal mantra by reflecting on a calming place using the five senses and crafting a Cinquain poem. The steps include describing the place, writing a poem about it, and using a synonym from the poem as a personal mantra. An example is provided, illustrating the process.

<u>Mantra</u>: A repeated word, aligned with your breath, used silently or aloud to focus the mind and foster calmness.

<u>Grounding Anchor Reflection</u>: Think of a real place that makes you feel calm, connected, grounded, and safe. Silently or in a journal describe your place using your five senses (visual, smell, touch, taste, & hear) and notice how you feel.

What do you see?
What do you touch or what textures, shapes, or colors stand out?
What do you hear?
What do you smell?
How does it make you feel?

<u>Journal</u>: Craft a five-line poem about your place:

Line 1: Write one noun that names your anchor
Line 2: Write two adjectives describing your anchor
Line 3: Write three verbs (often ending in 'ing') that bring your anchor to life
Line 4: Write a four-word phrase that reflects your feelings
Line 5: Write one synonym (closely associated word) for your anchor that sums up your experience

<u>Personal Mantra</u>: Use the word from Line 5: _____.

Example:
Anchor: Chair

Poem
Chair
Blue, comfortable
Supporting, elevating, relaxing
Nestled in plush coziness
Ease

Mantra
"Ease"

Using Your Personal Mantra to Cultivate Inner Calmness

A personal mantra can be a powerful tool to reset your mind, refocus your energy, and restore balance. The word or short phrase serves to ground and calm—a simple yet meaningful guide for navigating life's chaos. The mantra, aligned with your breath, can help you foster calmness and clarity. Below are five steps to help you incorporate your personal mantra into your daily life:

1. Choose Your Mantra with Intention. Select a word or short phrase that deeply resonates with you. For this book's framework, your mantra is the final word of your poem. It should embody your desired sense of grounding, balance, or focus. Examples include "peace," "strength," or "calm."

2. Find a Quiet Moment. Take a few moments in a space where you feel comfortable and uninterrupted. You can sit or stand, close your eyes if it feels natural, and begin to turn your focus inward. If you're in a busy or noisy environment, take a few slow, deep breaths to center yourself before continuing.

3. Align Your Mantra with Your Breath. Silently or softly, repeat your mantra in rhythm with your breath. On an inhale, think or say your mantra to yourself. On the exhale, imagine releasing tension or anything that no longer serves you. Alternatively, inhale positivity and exhale the mantra itself. Explore which pattern feels most grounding for you. Let the repetition create a calming cadence in your mind.

4. Feel Its Presence. As you repeat your mantra, focus on the sensations it evokes. Let its meaning settle into your thoughts and body. For example, if your mantra is "peace," imagine a wave of peaceful energy spreading through you with every breath. Allow this connection to deepen with each repetition. Perhaps you begin your mantra practice with 3-5 iterations and work your way up to 3-5 minutes.

5. Revisit Your Mantra Throughout the Day. Your mantra is not limited to moments of meditation. Return to it anytime you need to recenter—whether during a stressful situation, while transitioning between tasks, or before bed. Even a few seconds of silently repeating your mantra can bring you back to a place of calm and focus.

APPENDIX D:
Color Coding

These color-coding suggestions offer a visually engaging layout. Feel free to use or explore your own coding ideas.

- ➢ Yoga and Breathwork: Blue (calm and grounding)
- ➢ Nature Immersion: Green (symbolizing growth and nature)
- ➢ Plant-based Eating: Orange (vitality and nourishment)
- ➢ Journaling: Yellow (inspiration and creativity)
- ➢ Prayer or Reflection: Purple (spirituality and mindfulness)
- ➢ Connection Activity: Red (love and social bonds)

APPENDIX E:
Humble Warrior Wellness & Yoga Nonprofit

Humble Warrior Wellness & Yoga nonprofit is a trusted and valued resource dedicated to supporting women veterans and women first responders through the transformative pillars of connection and holistic wellness and has become a beacon of support for countless women who serve and protect. Since its founding, Humble Warrior has been at the forefront of providing unique, no-cost wellness retreats, workshops, and virtual programs, designed specifically for women who have given so much to their communities and country. With an all-volunteer board, the organization has established a reputation for care and connection.

Mission-Driven Wellness for Women Veterans and First Responders

At the heart of Humble Warrior's work is its mission: to provide holistic wellness services to women veterans and women first responders that cultivate enhanced well-being and reduce social isolation. The nonprofit's board members understand firsthand the challenges faced by women in these roles. Raquel Durden, U.S. Army combat veteran and Chair; Mary Beth Wheeler, U.S. Air Force combat veteran and Vice Chair; and Katie Lovely, U.S. Army combat veteran and Secretary—all seasoned practitioners of holistic wellness—use their shared experience to guide the organization in delivering innovative programs. With the support of Treasurer Stacy Wilson, military family member, and Communications Coordinator Gabrielle Draxler, U.S. Army veteran, Humble Warrior is committed to building a strong sense of community for women who serve.

A Holistic Approach to Wellness: Retreats and More!

Humble Warrior's wellness retreats are at the core of the organization's programming. Annually, they host a Newcomer's Wellness Retreat—a transformative experience for women new to Humble Warrior's community. Participants explore guided journaling sessions, yoga, meditation, plant-based eating demonstrations, and nature-centric activities, all designed to foster self-discovery and renewal. Alumni of Humble Warrior's retreats are invited to participate in more advanced holistic wellness workshops and retreats that feature mindful art projects, sound bath sessions, essential oil use, and more. These immersive experiences allow participants to deepen their wellness practices and sustain the benefits of self-care and connection long after the retreat ends.

Many of the women who attend Humble Warrior's programs express deep gratitude for the impact these experiences have had on their lives. Sasha, who attended a recent retreat, shares, "Thank you for a great event and a new way to look at the future." Another participant, Asti, reflecting on her experience, shares, "Thanks for a fabulous day! I will never be able to tell you all how much it meant for me to be there. My life is truly renewed and replenished by the experience!" These powerful testimonials illustrate the life-changing impact Humble Warrior has on its participants. After years of hypervigilance, we introduce strategies to help them dial down.

Expanding Beyond the Retreat: Virtual Communities and Programs

In addition to in-person retreats and workshops, Humble Warrior Wellness & Yoga, Inc. has expanded its reach through its vibrant online communities. On social media and YouTube, the organization offers virtual yoga classes, guided wellness practices, and other resources, allowing women veterans and first responders to stay connected no matter where they are. One of the most beloved virtual programs is the Sip 'n Read Sisters Book Club, led by co-facilitators Tammy Norton and Robin Hemmer, which has met monthly online for the past five years. This virtual gathering of like-minded women provides a space for reflection, discussion, and the chance to win a surprise wellness care package sent directly to the winner's home. It's not just about the books—it's about the connection that forms when women share stories and insights together, even from afar. The book club is just one of the many ways Humble Warrior strives to create a sense of belonging and support, even for those who may not be able to attend in-person retreats. Whether it's through an online class or a workshop, the message is clear: Humble Warrior is here for all women veterans and first responders, wherever they may be.

For a free, certified yoga teacher-led class, visit our Humble Warrior Wellness & Yoga YouTube:

Excellent descriptions of commonly used yoga poses are available on our Humble Warrior Wellness & Yoga website's Yoga Pose Directory.

For additional information, visit the Humble Warrior website:

Looking Forward: The Next Chapter for Humble Warrior

Through its emphasis on wellness and community, Humble Warrior Wellness & Yoga, Inc. has created a space where women veterans and first responders can come together to grow and connect. The future holds even more exciting opportunities to support women who serve. The nonprofit is committed to building a legacy of connection and wellness for women veterans and first responders, helping them thrive on their unique journeys. The organization relies on grants, gifts, and donations to fund its life-changing programs. Visit humblewarrior.org to connect, volunteer, and donate.

References

Chapter 2: The Power of Connections

Centers for Disease Control and Prevention. 2024, May 15. "Health Effects of Social Isolation and Loneliness." Centers for Disease Control and Prevention. https://www.cdc.gov/social-connectedness/risk-factors/index.html
Psychological Association. 2024, October 22. "Manage Stress: Strengthen your Support Network." American Psychological Association. https://www.apa.org/topics/stress/manage-social-support
Shovestul, B., Han, J., Germine, L., & Dodell-Feder, D. 2020. "Risk Factors for Loneliness: The High Relative Importance of Age Versus other Factors." PLoS ONE, 15(2), e0229087. https://doi.org/10.1371/journal.pone.0229087

Chapter 3: Breathe In, Let Go

Kalaivani, S., Kumari, M. J., & Pal, G. K. 2019. "Effect of Alternate Nostril Breathing Exercise on Blood Pressure, Heart Rate, and Rate Pressure Product among Patients with Hypertension in JIPMER, Puducherry." *Journal of Education and Health Promotion*, 8, 145. https://doi.org/10.4103/jehp.jehp_32_19
Ma, X., Yue, Z. Q., Gong, Z. Q., Zhang, H., Duan, N. Y., Shi, Y. T., Wei, G. X., & Li, Y. F. 2017. "The Effect of Diaphragmatic Breathing on Attention, Negative Affect, and Stress in Healthy Adults." *Frontiers in Psychology*, 8, 874. https://doi.org/10.3389/fpsyg.2017.00874
Woodyard, C. 2011. "Exploring the Therapeutic Effects of Yoga and its Ability to Increase Quality of Life." *International Journal of Yoga*, Jul;4(2):49-54. doi: 10.4103/0973-6131.85485. PMID: 22022122; PMCID: PMC3193654. https://pmc.ncbi.nlm.nih.gov/articles/PMC3193654/

Chapter 4: Nature's Reset Button

"Calm" 2012. https://www.calm.com
Jo, H., Song, C., & Miyazaki, Y. 2019. "Physiological Benefits of Viewing Nature: A Systematic Review of Indoor Experiments." *International Journal of Environmental Research and Public Health*, 16(23), 4739. https://doi.org/10.3390/ijerph16234739
Chevalier G. 2015. "The Effect of Grounding the Human Body on Mood." *Psychological Reports*, 116(2), 534–542. https://doi.org/10.2466/06.PR0.116k21w5

Li, Q. 2010. "Effect of Forest Bathing Trips on Human Immune Function." *Environmental Health and Preventive Medicine*, 15(1), 9–17. https://doi.org/10.1007/s12199-008-0068-3

Li, Q. 2018. *Forest Bathing: How Trees can Help you Find Health and Happiness.* Viking.

Louv, R. 2005. *Last Child in the Woods: Saving our Children from Nature-deficit Disorder.* Algonquin Books.

Ober, C., Sinatra, S. T., & Zucker, M. 2010. "Earthing: the Most Important Health Discovery Ever?" Laguna Beach, CA, *Basic Health Publications*.

Chapter 5: Eating for Energy and Clarity

Craig, W. J., & Mangels, A. R. 2009. "Position of the American Dietetic Association: Vegetarian Diets." *Journal of the American Dietetic Association*, 109(7), 1266–1282. https://pubmed.ncbi.nlm.nih.gov/19562864/

Environmental Working Group. 2024. "Clean 15 List." Accessed from https://www.ewg.org/foodnews/clean-fifteen.php

Environmental Working Group. 2024. "Dirty Dozen List." Accessed from https://www.ewg.org/foodnews/dirty-dozen.php

Food and Drug Administration & Environmental Protection Agency. 2021, October. "Advice about Eating Fish." Accessed from https://www.fda.gov/fishadvice

Fulkerson, L., et al. 2011. *Forks over Knives.* [Santa Monica, CA]: [New York, NY], Monica Beach Media.

Greger, M. 2015. *How not to Die.* Flatiron Books.

Greger, M. 2019. *Dr. Greger's Daily Dozen* https://apps.apple.com/us/app/dr-gregers-daily-dozen/id1060700802

Hunt, J. R. 2003. "Bioavailability of Iron, Zinc, and Other Trace Minerals from Vegetarian Diets." *American Journal of Clinical Nutrition*, 78(3 Suppl), 633S–639S. https://pubmed.ncbi.nlm.nih.gov/12936958/

Massey Cancer Center. 2018. "Diet and Nutrition: Eat the Rainbow." Accessed from https://www.masseycancercenter.org/news/diet-and-nutrition-eat-the-rainbow/

Matsuyama, S., Shimazu, T., Tomata, Y., Zhang, S., Abe, S., Lu, Y., & Tsuji, I. 2022. "Japanese Diet and Mortality, Disability, and Dementia: Evidence from the Ohsaki Cohort Study." *Nutrients,* 14(10), 2034. https://doi.org/10.3390/nu14102034

National Oceanic and Atmospheric Administration. 2024, June. "What is the Biggest Source of Pollution in the Ocean?" Accessed from https://oceanservice.noaa.gov/facts/pollution.html

Sofi, F., Cesari, F., Abbate, R., Gensini, G. F., & Casini, A. 2008. "Adherence to Mediterranean Diet and Health Status: Meta-analysis." *BMJ* (Clinical research ed.), 337, a1344. https://doi.org/10.1136/bmj.a1344

Tortora, G. J., & Derrickson, B. 2017. *Principles of Anatomy and Physiology* (15th ed.). John Wiley & Sons.

Turner-McGrievy, G. M., Barnard, N. D., Cohen, J., Jenkins, D. J., Gloede, L., & Green, A. A. 2015. "A Plant-based Diet for Overweight and Obesity Prevention and Treatment." *Journal of Geriatric Cardiology*, 12(5), 369-382. https://www.ncbi.nlm.nih.gov/pmc/articles/PMC5466943/

Chapter 6: Journal Your Way to Peace

Doran, G. T. 1981. "There's a SMART Way to Write Management's Goals and Objectives." *Management Review*, 70(11), 35-36.

Emmons, R. A., & McCullough, M. E. 2003. "Counting Blessings Versus Burdens: An Experimental Investigation of Gratitude and Subjective Well-being in Daily Life." *Journal of Personality and Social Psychology*, 84(2), 377-389. https://doi.org/10.1037/0022-3514.84.2.377

Frattaroli, J. 2006. "Experimental Disclosure and its Moderators: A Meta-analysis." *Psychological Bulletin*, 132(6), 823-865.

Locke, E. A., & Latham, G. P. 2002. "Building a Practically Useful Theory of Goal Setting and Task Motivation: A 35-year Odyssey." *American Psychologist*, 57(9), 705-717.

Pennebaker, J. W., & Chung, C. K. 2007. "Expressive Writing, Emotional Upheavals, and Health." *Journal of Clinical Psychology*, 55(1), 1-7.

Smyth, J. M. 1998. "Written Emotional Expression: Effect Sizes, Outcome Types, and Moderating Variables." *Journal of Consulting and Clinical Psychology*, 66(1), 174-184.

Smyth, J. M., Hockemeyer, J. R., & Tulloch, H. 2010. "Expressive Writing and Post-traumatic Stress Disorder: Effects on Trauma Symptoms, Mood States, and Cortisol Reactivity." *British Journal of Health Psychology*, 13(1), 85-93.

Chapter 7: Prayer Power

Buettner, D., & Skemp, S. 2016. "Blue Zones: Lessons from the World's Longest Lived." *American Journal of Lifestyle Medicine*, 10(5), 318-321. https://doi.org/10.1177/1559827616637066

Chen, Y., & VanderWeele, T. J. 2018. "Associations of Religious Upbringing with Subsequent Health and Well-being from Adolescence to Young Adulthood: An Outcome-wide Analysis." *American Journal of Epidemiology*, 187(11), 2355-2364. https://doi.org/10.1093/aje/kwy142

The Good Way. n.d. "A Daily Practice of Prayer Guide." Accessed from
    https://thegoodway.live/resources/prayer/a-daily-practice-of-prayer-guide
Levine, E. G., Aviv, C., Yoo, G., Ewing, C., & Au, A. 2009. "The Benefits of
    Prayer on Mood and Well-being of Breast Cancer
    Survivors. *Supportive Care in Cancer*, 17, 295–306.
    https://doi.org/10.1007/s00520-008-0482-5

Appendix A: The Eight Limbs of Yoga Overview

Satchidananda, S. 2012. "The Yoga Sutras of Patanjali: Translation and
    Commentary" (Revised edition). *Integral Yoga Publications.*

Appendix B: Types of Yoga

Miller, R., et al. 2021. "Yoga Meditation for Active Duty Military Members
    with Post-traumatic Stress Disorder: Results and Discussion of a
    Landmark Initial Study." *Journal of Alternative and Complementary
    Medicine*, 27(6), 522. https://doi.org/10.1089/acm.2020.0466

DISCUSSION PROMPTS

Personal Reflection and Growth Questions

1. What was your biggest takeaway from *Dial Down*?

2. Which chapter resonated most with you, and why?

3. How did personal stories and interviews impact your understanding of holistic wellness?

4. The book highlights the importance of storytelling as a healing tool. How can sharing your story contribute to your wellness and inspire others?

5. How does this book challenge or reinforce your understanding of self-care and wellness?

6. How can holistic wellness practices create ripple effects in families or communities?

7. Which practices do you believe are most impactful for individuals in high-stress or service-oriented professions?

Personal Application and Group Activity

1. What does the phrase "turning inward to find calm" mean to you, and how can it shape your response to future challenges?

2. Share the poem you created using the Cinquain poem framework and personal one-word mantra. What insights did you gain in writing it?

3. Discuss ways the group can support each other in implementing the strategies from the book in their daily lives.

ACKNOWLEDGEMENTS

This book is a passion project whose seeds were planted during the social-distancing isolation of the COVID-19 pandemic. Like so many others, I found myself searching for something meaningful to explore in forced isolation. In stillness, I could reflect, write, and create. As the world faced a surge in mental health challenges during the pandemic, the demand for holistic wellness services grew significantly. It was during this time that the idea for *Dial Down* began to take shape as my personal passion project. I wholeheartedly believe God orchestrated every step of this journey. I thank Him for placing the people, resources, and opportunities I needed directly in my path. From the idea to the interviews, from the framework to the final chapters, I have felt God's hand on this process.

I am deeply grateful to my core editing team, Valerie (Val) Havill and Teresa Ramsey, whose complementary talents shaped this manuscript into what it is today. Val's thoughtful feedback and encouragement helped me dig deep into my research and refine my content. Teresa's keen editorial eye ensured that every word found its proper place, while her guidance helped me stay true to my voice. Together, they made this manuscript clearer, stronger, and more impactful.

I have immense gratitude and thanks to my publishing team at Fresh Water Press! This triad of incredible women publishers brought to life the very best version of my manuscript and amplified my message of connection and wellness to a wider audience by publishing my book. Thank you to Sophia Dramm for her creative and responsive marketing. Thank you to Vagabond Creative Studio for designing a gorgeous cover that captured the quintessential moment between chaos and inner calm.

To my husband, I thank you for your unwavering support, encouragement, and feedback throughout this endeavor. You reminded me this book would be a meaningful, practical resource for many readers.

A heartfelt thank you to the incredible staff and the volunteers who have served on the Humble Warrior Wellness & Yoga, Inc Board of Directors. Your leadership, generosity, and kindness have left a lasting impact on the organization. Thank you to Diane Flowers, Carmen Morales, Teresa Ramsey, Claire Williams, Stacy Wilson, Suzy Willis, Katie Duke, Mary Beth Wheeler, Gabrielle Draxler, Amanda Avalos, and Amy DeLira.

To the many individuals who graciously shared their stories, experiences, and expertise for this book, thank you! Your willingness to be vulnerable and authentic enriched these pages and brought the heart of this project to life.

Finally, to every reader, I hope this book inspires you to turn inward and discover the practices that bring calm and balance to your life. May it remind you of the strength and beauty found in connection with others, nature, and God.

ABOUT THE AUTHOR

Raquel Durden is an honorably retired U.S. Army Lieutenant Colonel with a distinguished military career, including combat service.

She is also a sought-after keynote speaker, workshop facilitator, consultant, and advocate for holistic wellness. Raquel has parlayed the lessons learned from her military service and her journey as an advanced-stage cancer survivor into a successful nonprofit supporting women who serve. Her organization, Humble Warrior Wellness & Yoga, Inc., a 501(c)(3) based in Georgia, was recognized as a 2024 finalist for a Greater Athens Area Foundation Nonprofit of the Year. Additionally, Raquel received the prestigious Georgia Woman Veteran of the Year 2025 award, a testament to her ongoing impact on the veteran and first responder communities.

Drawing from her personal experiences, Raquel empowers others to navigate challenges and embrace calm through holistic practices like yoga, breathwork, and community connection. She lives in Georgia with her husband, Dave, a retired combat veteran who completed five deployments to Afghanistan, and their two rescue dogs, Radar and Grace.

When she's not writing or leading wellness initiatives, you can find Raquel at her desk with Grace, her spirited writing companion. Grace often places her paws on Raquel's chair as a gentle reminder to take breaks, find balance, and keep calm. Raquel's ability to merge strength with humor and resilience with compassion inspires all who meet her. Raquel's poetry has been published in *Harvest International's Out of Many One* (2004).

Ideal Speaker for Your Next Event

Whether addressing a conference, corporate event, or community gathering, Raquel's dynamic storytelling and actionable insights make her an ideal speaker for your next event. She engages audiences on topics ranging from leadership and wellness to overcoming adversity.

Stay Connected!

Instagram: @raquelmdurden
Facebook: @raquel.durden
Email: info@raqueldurden.com

In a Book Club? Raquel can create a video to kick off your group's discussion.

The Fresh Water Press was founded February 2024 in Two Rivers, Wisconsin, and specializes in books by writers who live in or write about the northeastern Wisconsin lakeshore. The Press publishes in several genres and welcomes submissions from underrepresented authors and unique voices.

Titles from Fresh Water Press:

Opening Nights: A Collection of Theater Stories

Ghost(ed) Woman & the Electric Purple Pants by Emilie Lindemann

Dial Down: Holistic Strategies to Move from Chaos to Calm by Raquel Durden

Radio Starr by Lisa Lehmann

www.ingramcontent.com/pod-product-compliance
Lightning Source LLC
Chambersburg PA
CBHW071117160426
43196CB00013B/2599